Christopher Wilder:

The True Story of The Beauty Queen Killer

by Jack Rosewood

**Historical Serial Killers and Murderers
True Crime by Evil Killers
Volume 16**

Copyright © 2016 by Wiq Media

ALL RIGHTS RESERVED

No part of this book may be reproduced, stored in a retrieval system, or transmitted in any form or by any means, electronic, mechanical, photocopying, recording, scanning, or otherwise, without the prior written permission of the publisher.

ISBN-13: 978-1533070302

DISCLAIMER:

This serial killer biography includes quotes from those closely involved in the case of American serial killer Christopher Bernard Wilder, and it is not the author's intention to defame or intentionally hurt anyone involved. The interpretation of the events leading up to Wilder' s 1984 murder spree and subsequent suicide are the author's as a result of researching the true crime murder. Any comments made about the psychopathic or sociopathic behavior of Wilder's are the sole opinion and responsibility of the person quoted.

Free Bonus!

**Get two free books when you sign up to my VIP newsletter at www.jackrosewood.com
150 interesting trivia about serial killers
and the story of serial killer Herbert Mullin.**

Contents

Introduction 1

CHAPTER 1: The Origins of the Beauty Queen Killer 5

    The Near Death Experiences 6

    The First Signs of Sickness 8

    The Sydney Gang-Rape 10

    An Attempt at Domesticity 13

CHAPTER 2: Wilder Moves to the United States 14

    Building a Fortune 14

    Sexual Assaults in the 1970s 16

    Back in Australia 21

CHAPTER 3: The Killing Spree 23

    Return to Florida 24

    The Miami Grand Prix 24

    Tying up Loose Ends 27

    Leaving Miami 31

    The FBI Focuses on Wilder 34

CHAPTER 4: Killing From Coast to Coast 39

    The Victims Begin to Pile Up 40

    Wilder Stays One Step Ahead of the FBI's Technology 46

    Getting More Brazen 49

    Tina Marie Risico 52

    Heading North 64

CHAPTER 5: Final Considerations 69

    What Drove the Beauty Queen Killer? 70

    Other Potential Victims 75

    The Wanda Beach Slayings 75

    More Possible Victims in Florida 78

    The Collector 84

Conclusion 87

A Note From The Author 104

Introduction

In the span of just over a month in the spring of 1984, Australian born entrepreneur and serial killer, Christopher Bernard Wilder, unleashed a bloody rampage on the United States that left at least nine women dead and three others brutalized. Wilder often approached his victims under the guise that he was a fashion photographer who could help the unsuspecting women get started in modeling. Once Wilder successfully lured a girl or young woman into his car with promises of stardom, he quickly went to work torturing, raping, and killing his quarry, which eventually earned him the moniker of the "beauty queen killer." While Wilder was in the middle of his spree no attractive teenage girl or young adult woman who came in contact with him was safe.

He especially loved to prowl shopping malls looking for unsuspecting young female victims, but he was also known to search for his victims in parking lots, college campuses, and convenience stores.

Wherever Wilder went he collected a new victim for his macabre collection.

As quickly as Wilder's spree began, it ended in dramatic fashion when the killer decided he would rather take his own life than be executed by the state or spend the remainder of his life in prison. Because Wilder died before trial, many mysteries persist concerning his motives, number of victims and even his classification as a true serial killer.

Perhaps what intrigues most about the case of the beauty queen killer is his social status before the 1984 killing spree. Serial killers have come from all socio-economic backgrounds, but few have been truly wealthy and most tend to be loners.

On the surface, Christopher Bernard Wilder was like few other serial killers: he was a wealthy self-made man who enjoyed the company of plenty of beautiful women and was well liked among his peers. But underneath this carefully crafted façade was a twisted individual who enjoyed hurting his fellow humans, especially women.

When it came to sadism, Christopher Wilder could compete with the best of them. Before killing his victims, Wilder often subjected them to hours and sometimes even days of torture that included rape, beatings, cutting, and electrocution by crudely created devices. Truly, Wilder was like two different people.

It appears that for a time, Wilder thought he could have it all: money, property, prestige, and women. For most of the 1970s and '80s Wilder lived the "good life" in southern Florida, but eventually his murderous impulses proved to be too hard for him to control and so he embarked on his cross country killing spree. As Wilder traveled from the east coast to the west coast and then back to the east coast he left nine dead and numerous more lives wrecked in his wake; but the police were nearly powerless to stop him!

Shortly after Wilder began his nationwide murder spree in Florida, local police and the FBI learned his identity, but unfortunately, due to the beauty queen killer's mobile nature and the limitations of 1980s technology, he was able to stay one step ahead of law enforcement.

Ultimately, the core of the Christopher Wilder story concerned not how the serial killer was able to cover his crimes up in order to evade law enforcement, but how he was able to keep moving and killing with constant media attention. Wilder became the focus of a national manhunt that placed him on the FBI's infamous "Top Ten" list and on the front pages of newspapers from coast to coast. The media attention seemed to aggravate the beauty queen killer, not slow him down, which presented a unique problem for the FBI. As Gordon McNeil, who was one of the lead FBI agents on the Wilder case, stated: "In this particular case we had an individual who was kidnaping, raping, torturing, and murdering a woman about every day and a half."

As Christopher Wilder drove across the United States, he stalked and hunted his human prey, but as he did so he in turn became the quarry of the FBI in one of the biggest and most exciting manhunts in American history.

CHAPTER 1:
The Origins of the Beauty Queen Killer

Christopher Bernard Wilder was born on March 13, 1945, in Sydney, Australia to an American naval officer father and an Australian mother. As the oldest of four brothers in the family, Wilder was looked to for support by his younger siblings and his parents, but he never seemed to care much for responsibility and his parents were always there to cover for him. Young Christopher Wilder was a spoiled child, which may be because life began so difficult for him.

The debate over whether a serial killer is born or created has been argued in the halls of academia and on popular television shows since the FBI first identified the category of "serial killer" in the late 1970s, with little resolution or either side budging from their stance. Those who believe serial killers are made point towards the unstable home environment and abuse that many serial killers suffered as children, while those who believe that some are just born to kill point out that not all serial killers grew up in abusive homes and in fact some had privileged, comfortable childhoods.

In many ways, Christopher Wilder's upbringing seems to support the argument that some people are born to kill. By all accounts his family life was stable, as there were no signs of abuse by the parents toward their children, and economically solid. The Wilders also had family and friends in both countries so there was definitely a support network.

The Wilder family enjoyed a solid, middle class life in Australia and the United States.

But despite the seemingly placid life of the Wilder family, young Christopher suffered two near death experiences that may have profoundly affected his philosophy on life.

The Near Death Experiences

A near death experience can be a life changing event for anyone who has one. The experience can be either positive or negative, depending on the individual and the intensity of the experience. Some people walk away from a near death experience with a sense of gratitude for having lived and set about to make positive changes in their lives.

Other people use near death experiences as a way to justify self-destructive behavior.

After surviving a near death encounter, some people see themselves as indestructible and so embark on heavy drug and alcohol binges and engage in risky sexual activity and criminality.

Christopher Wilder had two near death experiences as a child that apparently pushed him in the direction of the second path.

Wilder's first brush with death came during his birth. He was born prematurely and the doctors believed so strongly that he would die that a priest was called to perform last rites. As the priest delivered the sacrament, his parents held a vigil through the night. The infant Wilder survived the ordeal, but was faced with another life or death situation a few years later.

As a child, young Christopher Wilder was like many of the boys his age in Australia: he liked to spend time with his friends at the beach swimming, fishing and generally enjoying the sunny climate of the southern hemisphere. On one normal, sunny day on the coast near Sydney, Wilder and his buddies went swimming like many other days previously, but when the young Wilder entered the water he disappeared.

Panic quickly set in with Wilder's friends when he did not surface. The young boy was under the water, drowning and perhaps close to death once more.

Wilder's friends and beach lifeguards were able to rescue Wilder from the ocean, but he almost died, which brought his total of near death experiences to two. Most people never have one near experience in a lifetime; but Christopher Wilder had two before he reached puberty, which may have played a role in how he viewed life and relations with other humans.

After he survived the drowning, Wilder was plagued with fainting episodes for the remainder of his youth, but more importantly, he appears to have taken a more reckless attitude towards life and began to display a lack of empathy towards other people, especially women.

The First Signs of Sickness

Most serial killers exhibit signs of their homicidal future at an early age. Some abuse and kill animals, while others invoke their sexual deviancies and murderous impulses on their peers. No matter if the future killer abused animals, other children or both as a child, one common thread seems to run through all of the cases – if caught as a child, the offender was treated lightly by the criminal justice system.

Christopher Wilder, like many other notorious serial killers from around the world, could not repress his sexual deviancy and so it was manifested in a number of ways during his childhood.

The future beauty queen killer displayed the first troubling signs of his sadistic future when he was caught window peeping in his Sydney neighborhood. Concerned neighbors called the police when they noticed someone lurking around their quiet suburban neighborhood, peeping in their windows; but when Wilder was apprehended and it was learned that he was a neighborhood boy, he was released to his parents with little more than a scolding.

The Australian authorities had the perfect opportunity to get Wilder the help he needed that would have possibly saved lives, but in the late 1950s such behavior was written off as boyish exuberance and sexual experimentation.

The police had no way of knowing that they had a future sexual sadist in their midst.

The local police and court systems were not the only people who refused to recognize the deviancy that was growing in the young Wilder. Christopher's parents sheltered their son from punishment as they would do numerous times before his 1984 killing spree. Whenever Wilder had problems, legal or financial, he returned to the familiarity and safety of his parents' home, who were always willing to help their son any way they could. One could even say that Wilder's parents enabled his bad behavior from an early age and continued to do so throughout his adult years.

After the window peeping incident, Wilder and his family returned to their quiet suburban life as though nothing had happened: his parents went on with their jobs and Christopher continued to advance through high school. To his parents, neighbors, and local authorities, it seemed as though Wilder would move on from his brief foray into juvenile delinquency, but the window peeping incident appeared to have the opposite effect.

Wilder's window peeping opened up a dark corner of his twisted personality.

The Sydney Gang-Rape

The window peeping incident should have been a sign to those close to Wilder that something was seriously wrong with the young man, but instead he was left alone to further indulge his sadistic sexual fantasies. The next major incident in Wilder's young life proved to be much more serious than window peeping, but unfortunately, the event was treated in much the same way by the authorities.

On a warm, sunny day in 1963 Wilder was spending his days much as he did at the time and in later years – hanging out at the beach with his friends admiring the bikini clad coeds who populated the seashore. Alone Wilder was truly a disturbed young man, but the group of friends he hung out with in 1963 appeared to be equally disturbed and it seems all of the young men fed on each other's problems and negativity.

As the day went by, Wilder and his friends began to consume copious amounts of alcohol, which then led to tough talk and bravado. After consuming more alcohol, the group then decided to find a female who could appease their sexual desires.

Wilder and his friends did not care if the female they found wanted to comply with their desires; they were going to take what they wanted!

Wilder and his buddies found an unfortunate teenage girl in an isolated part of the beach. At first, the young men tried to coax the girl into having consensual sex with them by offering her alcohol and complimenting her and when that did not work they eventually threatened her and then physically overwhelmed the frightened girl. Wilder and his friends all took turns raping the young girl and then left her on the beach, like discarded trash, when they were done.

The girl immediately went to the local police after her ordeal.

Since Wilder and his friends were a regular fixture on the Sydney beach scene they were all quickly arrested and prosecuted; but sentences for serious crimes in Australia were much different in the early 1960s then they are today.

Once more, Wilder's parents came to his aid in order to mitigate any possible prison sentence because he was then an adult under Australian law. The prosecutors and judge saw Wilder's familial support as a point in his favor along with the fact that he had no criminal record and so only gave the young man probation, with one important stipulation.

Wilder would have to undergo electroshock treatment.

Today, most people outside of the mental health profession have little knowledge of electroshock therapy other than what they may have seen in movies such as *One Flew Over the Cuckoo's Nest*. Most mental health professionals also have little experience with the controversial treatment method as it has been discredited by a plethora of doctors and academics and has been banned in some places.

But in the early 1960s electroshock therapy was considered a legitimate treatment method in most places throughout the world.

Wilder was given multiple electroshock treatments, which has led some to wonder if that was the actual trigger that caused him to go on his 1984 killing spree. It seems unlikely that the electroshock treatment alone caused him to kill because many people who also had the treatment never killed and on the other hand, most serial killers have never had electroshock treatment. Perhaps the most interesting connection between Wilder's electroshock therapy and his 1984 killing spree is the fact that he electrocuted many of his victims before killing them.

Perhaps Wilder electrocuted his victims in order to make them feel the pain he felt in the 1960s as a type of revenge against the world, or maybe he was impressed with the process. Whatever the reasons, it is significant that electricity played a role in attempts to treat him and as a method he used to torture many of his victims.

After Wilder's gang-rape conviction he kept a low profile for the rest of the 1960s and apparently suppressed his sadistic urges for a while.

An Attempt at Domesticity

As Wilder's family covered for him on more than one occasion, they also tried to do what they could to help him establish normalcy. His father helped him find work and both his parents tried to find him a suitable mate. Wilder finally responded to his family's pleas for him to settle into a normal, law abiding life when he married a woman in 1968. But Wilder's problems were far too deep seated for a marriage to solve. Wilder quickly unleashed his sexually sadistic fantasies on his bride, who then promptly left him after only a week of marriage.

The future beauty queen killer was a failure at marriage and his opportunities in Australia seemed exhausted, not to mention that he was on the Sydney police's radar for his sex offenses.

It was time for Wilder to make a move.

CHAPTER 2:
Wilder Moves to the United States

For many normally adjusted people, a move can be a good way to recharge one's life, a way to start fresh without some of the hindrances or bad influences. A move can be a good chance for someone to move ahead in his/her career, start a new career, or just get a much needed change in scenery.

In 1969 Christopher Bernard Wilder decided to take advantage of his dual citizenship by emigrating from Australia to the United States. Wilder arrived in Florida, which is where he lived until his infamous 1984 killing spree, and immediately immersed himself in the sun, sand, and sex that permeated the state at the time.

Wilder's move to the United States proved to be socially and financially beneficial for him, but a nightmare for numerous American women.

Building a Fortune

Wilder quickly became a fixture in south Florida's social and economic scene as he could be found at trendy bars and nightclubs with an assortment of women and he quickly began to amass a small fortune through a combination of shrewd investments and hard work.

Although most of the 1970s was marked by a weak dollar that eventually led to inflation and an oil crisis in the middle and later years of the decade, real estate values went up during the decade and eventually peaked with the return of the dollar during the 1980s. Wilder used some money that he had saved in Australia to buy some cheap land in Florida that eventually netted him a nice profit. Wilder was well on his way to becoming a wealthy man and it seems that he finally found something legal in which he was successful.

Wilder then created two different contracting companies that also proved to be quite lucrative. With the profits from his land deals and contracting companies, Wilder was able to buy a beachfront home and several "toys" that included: boats, motorcycles, and high performance sports cars. Wilder eventually turned his love of sports cars into a hobby and part-time profession as he raced competitively up until the time of his murder spree. Eventually, Wilder amassed a fortune that was worth over $2 million upon his death in 1984, which puts him in an exclusive category among serial killers as few were as wealthy when they carried out their acts.

Most people who amass similar amounts of wealth think ahead to the future and set aside amounts for their children or others; but Wilder lacked empathy, had no children, and was essentially myopic in his world view. The future beauty queen killer was a person who "lived in the moment" and used his wealth to live a lifestyle that revolved around his two favorite interests: cars and women.

Sexual Assaults in the 1970s

Like his adolescence in Australia, Wilder's life in Florida during the 1970s proved to be a prelude of more brutal things to come and should have been a wakeup call to the Florida authorities. But like in Australia, Wilder largely avoided any criminal sanctions for his crimes because either his victims refused to testify, or the authorities deemed that his acts were not serious enough to prosecute.

The Florida authorities did not know they had a monster in their midst.

But an examination of Wilder's life reveals that few people would have believed he was a sexual sadist; he was after all an honest, tax paying citizen who employed dozens of local residents.

How could Christopher Wilder be a killer, or even a sexual sadist?

The question is even more intriguing when one considers the context of Wilder's 1970s sexual assault spree.

Florida in 1969, much like other major metropolitan areas across the United States, was awash in the sexual revolution.

"Free love" became a part of the American lexicon as young people shattered traditional sexual norms by engaging in promiscuity along with other sexual behaviors once considered taboo.

Wilder was a reasonably attractive man with plenty of resources, so he should not have had a difficult time finding consensual sexual partners in 1970s Florida. And by all accounts he had plenty of girlfriends, which indicates that his sexual impulses came from a deeper, darker part of his soul.

Not long after Wilder arrived in Florida, he claimed his first American victim. He approached a young attractive nurse with a line that became a regular part of his *modus operandi*: Wilder told the woman that he was a professional photographer and that he could take some free photos of her in order to help get her modeling career started. The woman agreed and, perhaps being swept up by the sexual revolution, also agreed to pose for some nude photos. After he had taken the photos, Wilder then threatened to go public with the photos unless the woman agreed to have sex with him. The nurse spurned Wilder's sexual extortion attempt and instead went to the local police.

Sexual extortion crimes are rarely reported and extremely difficult to prosecute, even with the ubiquitous nature of technology today. In 1969, without any concrete evidence, Florida authorities were skeptical of the young nurse's claims and quickly wrote the incident off as either a lover's quarrel or as a woman who got more than she bargained for from a hippy free love session.

For the time being, Wilder was free to engage in more sexual sadism.

The next known case of sexually sadistic behavior committed by Wilder came in 1971 in Pompano Beach, Florida. In the Pompano Beach case, Wilder used his M.O. to entice two teenage girls to pose nude for him. The girls reported him to the local police, who arrested him for soliciting, but the charges were later dropped when the girls refused to testify in court.

Later that same year Wilder was arrested for forcing a teenage girl to give him oral sex, but once more the charges were dropped when the victim refused to testify.

As the 1970s progressed, Wilder seemed to have gotten bolder in his sexual assaults as he began to prey on multiple victims simultaneously.

In Wilder's next sexual assault, he employed another tactic that became part of his M.O. – drugging his victims. Wilder met a teenage girl in 1974 who he promised to make famous, but he instead drugged and raped the helpless girl. The girl, like the other Florida victims, went to the local authorities who prosecuted the predator to the fullest extent of the law.

Unfortunately for the women of Florida, the fullest extent of the law was not much in 1974. During the 1970s, the crime rate in the United States was skyrocketing and so politicians took a "get tough on crime" stance by increasing penalties for most crimes.

But the legal process works slowly and Wilder was sentenced under older, more lenient guidelines and so he was only given probation. The aphorism, "the wheels of justice turn slowly" clearly applies in this case and even more so when one considers the wider social context. Although lawmakers were taking a get tough on crime approach, it often takes months or years for bills to pass through state legislatures and become laws. Wilder had the advantage of operating within the "window" of the period when the laws were changing, but not yet applicable. He also apparently felt a sense of invulnerability as he had committed numerous serious sexual crimes on two continents but had not spent one day in prison.

Wilder was next charged with sexual battery in 1977 in a case where he admitted that he sexually assaulted a sixteen year old girl who he had lured into his car. He was quickly arrested because the girl was the daughter of one of his clients.

He claimed to the court that he was "down in the dumps" the day he committed the crime and that he was sorry for his actions. A psychologist who testified for the defense stated that he believed Wilder was not dangerous, but that he should be required to attend treatment.

He was acquitted by a jury after only fifty five minutes of deliberation.

The future beauty queen killer found himself in court once more in 1980 for sexual battery. The details of the case were eerily similar to many of Wilder's prior and subsequent cases: he conned two cute teenage girls with the promise of stardom if they would let him take their pictures. The two girls agreed and when the photo session was over, Wilder raped the one he liked best. He was able to plea bargain the charge down to attempted sexual battery and was given five years probation and ordered to see a psychologist. Records show that Wilder attended all of his required therapy sessions until he went on his killing spree.

Wilder was untouchable!

The beauty queen killer's last known sexual assault in his 1970s string came in 1980 in Boynton Beach, Florida. The case proved to be one of his most disturbing assaults as he forced two girls, ages ten and twelve, to perform oral sex on him. Although the girls reported the assault at the time, Wilder never came up as a suspect until after his killing spree became public when the girls recognized him on news reports. If successfully prosecuted under today's laws, Wilder would have faced a potential life sentence in prison and lifetime registration in a sex offender database.

But Wilder was able to take advantage of more lenient laws and dual citizenship to evade justice in Florida and travel back to Australia.

Back in Australia

Although Wilder was able to amass a nice fortune during the 1970s, he also managed to compile a criminal record and make himself known to the authorities in several different jurisdictions in Florida.

That was the reason he left Australia in the first place and why he returned to the familiar confines of Sydney not long after he sexually assaulted the two girls in Boynton Beach. Wilder moved back in with his parents who once more enabled their troubled son. They helped him find work and tried to steer him towards worthwhile, positive pursuits, but he quickly fell back into his old routines of window peeping and stalking girls on the Sydney beaches.

At this point it is unknown how many victims Wilder claimed in Australia during the early 1980s, but in 1982 he was arrested for sexual assault once more.

On a warm, sunny day in 1982 Wilder spent the day cruising the local malls and beaches for victims. Finally, he spied two attractive girls that he enticed with his standard line of taking free photos for their modeling portfolios. The girls agreed and went with Wilder to a remote location.

Once the three arrived at the isolated photo shoot, Wilder told the girls that they should take some nude shots and when they declined, he threatened to kill them. Wilder took a number of nude photos of the girls and then allowed them to leave relatively unharmed. The two girls immediately called the police who quickly arrested Wilder.

Wilder had escaped lengthy prison sentences on two different continents during the 1960s and '70s, but by the 1980s the get tough on crime stance prevailed among politicians and lawmakers not just in the United States, but also in Australia.

Wilder was looking at doing serious prison time for assaulting the two fifteen year old girls.

The beauty queen killer knew that he could not go to prison. Some people are made for prison, but not Christopher Bernard Wilder, so he appealed to his enabling parents for help once more, who promptly posted $350,000 bond for his release awaiting trial. Wilder thanked his dutiful parents by absconding from his bail, which left his parents on the hook for the remainder of the bail.

Wilder returned to Florida, never to see again his country of birth.

CHAPTER 3:
The Killing Spree

One of the factors that would help facilitate Wilder on his 1984 killing spree was the limited technology that law enforcement had at their disposal. Teletype helped relay information quickly, but it did not automatically enter that information into a database. Fingerprints had to be checked individually as there were no computer programs that could search for matches and DNA testing was still nearly a decade in the future.

These same technology limitations may have also helped Wilder travel so freely between Australia and the United States.

Although Wilder had dual citizenship and would have been able to travel freely between the United States and Australia even with criminal convictions, current technology would result in him being flagged if trying to leave the country while awaiting trial. This lack of technology allowed Wilder to simply get on a Qantas flight from Sydney to the United States where he quickly resumed his predatory lifestyle.

Return to Florida

Once Wilder returned to southern Florida he quickly picked up where he left off by investing in more land, hitting the nightclub scene, racing cars, and most importantly, hunting for new victims.

Wilder's sexual assault case in Australia was postponed several times, but as 1982 turned to '83 the case began to exert noticeable stress on the killer. He knew that if found guilty, he would more than likely go to prison, which was something the sadistic playboy never planned to do.

Wilder's impending case in Australia ultimately became the source of doom for nine American women.

The Miami Grand Prix

In February 1983, Miami area sports car racing enthusiasts came together to create the inaugural Miami Grand Prix. The event, which attracted thousands of racers and fans from around the world, was held in Miami's Bayfront Park. The first race proved to be successful enough in terms of advertising revenue, participants, and fan involvement that a second race was planned for 1984. Among the scores of participants in the February 26, 1984, race was Christopher Wilder.

Wilder finished the race in seventeenth place, which put him in the money with a cash prize of $400. Witnesses who were at the race reported that Wilder seemed extremely happy with his finish and even gloated a bit, but now it appears that Wilder went to the race to indulge his sadistic urges as much as his auto racing hobby.

On the day of the second annual Miami Grand Prix, Rosario Gonzalez was a beautiful, vivacious twenty year old Cuban-American woman. Gonzalez had done some minor modeling jobs before the Grand Prix and on the day of the second annual race she was there distributing free aspirin samples for one of the race's sponsors.

Rosario Gonzalez went missing on February 26 and her body was never found.

The exact details of Gonzalez's disappearance and presumed murder are not known to law enforcement officials because Wilder died before he could tell them anything, but it is believed that she was the beauty queen killer's first victim in his 1984 killing spree. Gonzalez and Wilder were believed to have met nearly two years prior and witnesses reported that Gonzalez was last seen with a man in a car that matched the description of one of Wilder's cars.

Although police are not sure, they can reasonably recreate what happened to the young woman based on his prior sexual assaults and subsequent assaults and murders.

After Wilder was done with his race, he was seen lurking around the park with his trademark camera and gear. He was clearly looking for a victim and unfortunately for Rosario Gonzalez, she became his quarry.

Wilder simply approached the young woman, complimented her on her looks, and then offered to do a free photo shoot with her to use for her portfolio. The beauty queen killer also had the advantage of being a race participant, which probably would have put Gonzalez more at ease with the predator. Wilder and Gonzalez were also believed to have been acquainted too and that helped to further place the young woman in the beauty queen killer's clutches.

After Wilder brought the young woman to an isolated location, he then proceeded to rape, torture, and murder her. He then disposed of her body in one of the thousands of canals or swamps of southern Florida. Wilder then moved on to his next victim.

But why did Wilder decide to start killing in 1984?

The answer to that question is not so simple and will be considered more thoroughly later, but it seems obvious that Wilder's criminality and pathology evolved as he got older. Wilder's criminal career began with window peeping as a child and culminated with murder at the age of thirty eight, but there were a lot of offenses in the years between and the nature of the offenses progressively got worse. Murder may have been the last bastion of sadism that Wilder had yet to cross, or perhaps, he simply murdered Gonzalez to keep her from going to the police. With a trial pending in Australia and a number of close calls for sexual assaults, the beauty queen killer may have seen Gonzalez as a loose end that needed to be dealt with. Whatever the reason for Wilder's murder of Gonzalez, Pandora's Box of murder was open; the beauty queen killer had crossed the Rubicon to become a homicidal sadist.

Tying up Loose Ends

Most of the most well-known and most prolific serial killers share a common theme in their victimology – they usually prey on strangers. Many serial killers found their victims in bars or working the streets so there could be a personal connection, but the connection is usually limited; the victims are rarely co-workers, neighbors, or family. For the most part, Christopher Wilder followed a similar victimology during his 1984 killing spree, with one exception – Elizabeth Kenyon.

In March 1984, Elizabeth Kenyon was a twenty three year old special education teacher in the Miami area. Family and friends described Kenyon as bright, warm, and the type of person who would help anyone who needed it. Kenyon was also very attractive as she was a Miss Florida finalist.

Elizabeth Kenyon was exactly the type of woman that Wilder found attractive.

Kenyon and Wilder briefly dated, but she ended the relationship after the beauty queen killer proposed to her. According to Kenyon's friends and family, Wilder was sexually aggressive and violent, which, along with their age difference, proved to be too much for Kenyon.

Elizabeth Kenyon was last seen on March 5, 1984.

Similar to the Gonzalez case, Kenyon's body was never discovered, but unlike the Gonzalez case, Kenyon's friends and family appealed to the local media and hired private investigators in order to identify and catch Elizabeth's killer.

Authorities believe that Wilder abducted, tortured, and murdered Kenyon all on the same day, as he did several times in the following weeks with some of his other victims. When Kenyon failed to report to her job the next day and when calls from her parents went unanswered, Elizabeth's parents called the police to report her missing.

The local police assured the Kenyon family that their daughter was probably just spending some time with friends, or perhaps she met a new boyfriend, and that she would turn up in a day or two. But when a couple of days passed, the Kenyons began to worry. Elizabeth's car was quickly located at the Miami international airport, which seemed to confirm to the local police that she had left town on a trip, but the Kenyons knew better.

Feeling frustrated with the local authorities, the Kenyon family turned to Miami area private detective Ken Whitaker and his son Ken Junior for answers.

The Whitakers quickly got to work on Elizabeth Kenyon's disappearance and were aided by a $50000 reward for information that the Kenyon family offered. In the end, it was not the monetary reward that helped identify Wilder as Kenyon's abductor but good old fashioned detective work by the Whitakers.

The Whitakers searched every inch of Elizabeth Kenyon's home for any clues about her whereabouts. Initially, the search revealed nothing special: there were no signs of drug use or criminal activity that usually contribute to a person's disappearance. The investigators then focused on Kenyon's photo albums because they noticed a man who was conspicuously present in many of the more recent pictures.

Upon asking family and friends of Elizabeth Kenyon who the mystery man was in the photos, the Whitakers were told it was Christopher Wilder, who then quickly became a person of interest in her disappearance. The Whitakers learned that Wilder had recently proposed marriage to Kenyon, but that she soundly denied his proposal. Believing that they possibly had a violent, spurned lover on their hands, the father-son detective team used their skills and knowledge to dig deeper into the case.

The Whitakers canvassed the area around Kenyon's work and home and soon learned that witnesses spotted Elizabeth with Wilder at a gas station near the school where she worked.

The Whitakers also discovered that Wilder was a consummate womanizer and possible serial sex offender.

After the Whitakers gave their report to the Kenyon family, it seemed clear to all parties involved that Christopher Bernard Wilder had something to do with Elizabeth's disappearance. The Kenyon family took the Whitakers' findings to the local police, but were once more met with skepticism and little help.

The Kenyon family decided to take matters into their own hands.

The Kenyon family believed that since local authorities in Florida were doing little to help find their daughter then they would appeal to a higher authority – the Federal Bureau of Investigation (FBI).

The FBI was formed in the early twentieth century to investigate violations of federal crimes. As the federal government has grown more laws have been added, which has meant that the FBI's role in American law enforcement has also increased. Some types of crimes that fall under the FBI's purview include the following: bank robbery, kidnapping (especially when the victim is transported across state lines), terrorism, and organized crime. Since the FBI is the federal government's primary law enforcement agency it has a large pool of resources, which is what the Kenyon family was counting on when they contacted the agency.

The Kenyons also contacted the local media.

After the Kenyons faced resistance from local law enforcement to investigate their daughter's disappearance, they had the Whitakers leak their report on the case to the *Miami Herald*. The *Herald* promptly published a story about Elizabeth's disappearance and although Wilder was never mentioned by name, it was stated that private investigators believed the culprit was an Australian born ex-boyfriend who fancied sports cars. The article also mentioned the disappearance of Rosario Gonzalez and stated that the private detectives believed the two cases were connected because Gonzalez was last seen at the race where the unnamed Australian also was.

The media exposure may have helped pique the FBI's interest in the case, but it also had the effect of driving the beauty queen killer underground.

Leaving Miami

In 1984, long before the internet became a ubiquitous part of daily life, most people read their city's daily newspaper. Wilder must have read the *Miami Herald* article about the Elizabeth Kenyon disappearance because he promptly left town without telling any of his friends or employees. In fact, when law enforcement authorities finally did search his home, they were surprised with how clean Wilder's home was. The home was too clean though as even Wilder's fingerprints could not be found.

Wilder's guilt was becoming apparent, but law enforcement could not locate the beauty queen killer.

The beauty queen killer packed his bags into one of his cars and then began traveling north along Interstate 95 on Florida's Atlantic coast. Wilder spent his birthday on March 13 in Daytona Beach, Florida, which is also where he claimed his next victim.

The details of Colleen Orsborn's abduction and murder remain murky because her body was not positively identified until 2011 and so for years her case was treated as a missing person and not one of Wilder's victims. Recently, circumstantial evidence has surfaced that firmly points toward Wilder as the killer: she fit the profile of one of Wilder's victims and the killer was registered at a Daytona Beach motel and checked out the day she disappeared on March 15.

Colleen Orsborn was a cute fifteen year old girl who was known to be friendly and gregarious, which is ultimately what got her killed. Wilder probably approached her at the local mall with his camera in hand and laid the same line on her as he did with all of his previous and subsequent victims. The world will never know how long Orsborn suffered at the beauty queen killer's hands, but it is clear that Wilder's murderous impulse could no longer be contained.

Wilder then drove south from Daytona Beach down Interstate 95 to Brevard County. The county is best known for being the home of the John F. Kennedy Space Center, which is situated on the north end of Merritt Island. The Space Center is located on the north end of the island, while most of the inhabitants reside on the south end.

The south end of Merritt Island is also home to the Merritt Square Mall.

The beauty queen killer stalked the mall on March 18, with his camera in hand, looking for a victim until he met twenty one year old Theresa Ferguson. Wilder impressed the young woman with a plethora of compliments and then offered to help the unsuspecting woman create a model portfolio.

Theresa Ferguson was never seen alive again.

Ferguson's body was recovered from a swampy area on the mainland across from Merritt Island in the unincorporated town of Canaveral Groves on March 23. Although Ferguson was missing for less than a week, the water, humidity, and warmth of Florida caused the corpse to start decaying, which led to complications with the autopsy. Authorities were later able to determine that Wilder beat Ferguson with a tire iron and then strangled her to death.

After killing Ferguson and disposing of her body, Wilder then went north to Jacksonville and west along Interstate 10.

The FBI Focuses on Wilder

The efforts of the Kenyon family to bring their daughter's killer to justice did not go unnoticed by the FBI. The FBI showed initial interest in the case when it was brought to their attention, but with no body they were not sure if a crime had even been committed and even if Wilder did kill Kenyon, murders are rarely investigated by the FBI and even more rarely prosecuted in federal court. Murders are sometimes prosecuted in federal court if it can be determined that the victim had his/her civil rights violated – as the Justice Department did during the 1960s in the successful prosecution of members of the Ku Klux Klan who beat state murder charges – or if the murder was part of a larger criminal conspiracy. The disappearance of Elizabeth Kenyon fit neither of those criteria, but the FBI was soon presented with evidence that allowed them to officially enter the investigation.

Rosario Gonzalez came from a tight-knit family, who like the Kenyon family, pleaded with local law enforcement to find their daughter. Unfortunately, also similar to the Kenyon case, their pleas fell on deaf ears. Once again it was the investigation by the Whitakers that raised the possibility that the disappearances of both women were probably connected. The publication of the Whitakers' findings in the *Miami Herald* also helped keep the case in the public eye where agents from the FBI were able to follow it.

"This connection drew my interest," said FBI agent Gordon McNeil. "I decided to open a preliminary kidnapping investigation to see if we had a violation of federal law."

The FBI would not have to wait long for Wilder to break a federal law.

Three days after the beauty queen killer left Merritt Island, he arrived in the state capital of Tallahassee and wasted no time finding his next victim. He took his camera to the Governor's Square Mall and began approaching attractive young women and girls about helping them land modeling jobs. Nineteen year old Linda Grover indicated interest in Wilder's proposal and agreed to go with him to a shooting location.

Once she got into Wilder's car things went badly for the attractive young blonde.

The beauty queen killer pulled out a Colt Python .357 revolver and threatened to kill Grover if she did not do what he demanded. Wilder then brought his victim across the state line to a motel in Georgia where he beat and brutally raped her.

He also superglued Grover's eyes shut.

The use of superglue on Grover was an aberration in Wilder's M.O. and it is unknown why he did so on this particular victim. It may have been that he was afraid of intimacy, even while he was in total control, and so glued Grover's eyes shut in order to hamper any possible deeper connection. It may also indicate that Wilder was feeling a sense of guilt at that point during his spree or possibly that he intended to let this victim live and thought that she would not be able to identify him if he glued her eyes shut. Grover may have also reminded Wilder of a woman he actually respected, such as his mother or another relative, and so he glued her eyes to keep from making eye contact.

Whatever the reason may have been, Grover was able to escape the beauty queen killer's clutches and later give a positive identification of him to the FBI.

When Wilder was not paying attention to her, Grover managed to loosen her bonds and then hide in the motel room's bathroom. Although there was no window in the bathroom, Grover screamed and yelled enough that Wilder became frightened and fled the scene.

Battered and bloodied, Grover was then discovered by motel staff who then contacted the authorities. Grover was brought to a local hospital where she was given a rape kit exam and then allowed to convalesce from her ordeal.

"I was in the hospital for a week or something like that," said Grover about her ordeal. "I had to basically leave the country while he was still a fugitive because they were concerned about my safety; they were concerned about my family's safety."

As she recovered in the hospital, the FBI asked Grover to identify her attacker from a photo lineup. Despite having her eyes glued shut for much of the attack, Grover was able to accurately identify Wilder from the lineup.

"It was absolutely no doubt in my mind, I mean I had spent hours with this person and that's who he was," said Grover on her identification of Christopher Wilder. "I just identified him as clearly Christopher Wilder."

As awful as the abduction, torture, and rape of Linda Grover was, it breathed new life into law enforcement's investigation of Christopher Wilder because she was kidnapped and brought across a state line, which firmly put the case under the purview of the FBI. With the full resources of the federal government now available to catch Wilder, many thought that the hunt would be over in a matter of hours, or days at the most.

But it seems that Wilder prepared for a cat and mouse game with the FBI.

Once the FBI was given full authority in the hunt for Christopher Wilder, they quickly got to work. One of the first things they did was to search his home for clues as to his whereabouts and the possibility of more victims. As mentioned above, Wilder thoroughly cleaned his home before he left, which perplexed FBI agents.

"There were basically no fingerprints left in Wilder's house. You're always going to find fingerprints inside a residence. It looked like everything had been totally cleaned," said Gordon McNeil about the initial stages of the FBI investigation.

The FBI also monitored his bank accounts and learned that he had withdrawn $19,000 before he left the Miami area. Although the resources that Wilder had at his disposal were nothing compared to the FBI's, they were enough for him to live on for a while and he also had a head start.

The FBI quickly put out an all-points bulletin (APB) across the teletype to all American law enforcement. The APB included a description of Wilder and his car, but the FBI realized that he possessed a cache of stolen license plates he was using to evade the police. "We never knew at the time what license plate he was using on that vehicle," said McNeil on the problem of locating Wilder's car.

Wilder had a good head start, but the hunt for the beauty queen killer had just begun.

CHAPTER 4:
Killing From Coast to Coast

After Wilder assaulted Linda Grover, he embarked on a cross country killing spree for the next three weeks that kept him one step ahead of the frustrated FBI. To this day his ultimate plan, if he had one, is unknown. It is believed that he was attempting to flee to Canada at the end of the spree, but before that he managed to cover thousands of miles across the United States in a trek that went from Florida to California and then from California to New Hampshire.

Did he have a target in California that he was unable to locate so he turned back east, or was he simply killing until he was caught? The fact that he nearly attempted to enter Canada would seem to indicate that he did not plan to get caught, but unfortunately, since Wilder is dead and left no written confession, we are left to guess.

What is known is that after Wilder assaulted Grover, he quickly put distance between himself and the state of Florida.

The Victims Begin to Pile Up

The day after Wilder assaulted Linda Grover, he was in Beaumont, Texas looking for his next victim. Beaumont was not the type of city that the playboy killer preferred: it is a gritty city located on the Gulf coast that grew in size and importance due to its many oil refineries and location next to the shipping lanes. Despite Beaumont's decidedly blue-collar background and the female population's more street smart attitude, the beauty queen killer eventually found a victim at the local mall.

After Wilder arrived in Beaumont, he went to the campus of Lamar University to hunt for his next victim. Along with the oil and shipping industries, Lamar University plays a vital role in Beaumont's economic and social life as it employs hundreds and over 15,000 students are enrolled. Many of Lamar's attractive female students are enrolled in the university's well-respected nursing program.

Walking Lamar's campus, the beauty queen killer was like a kid in a candy store.

But Wilder quickly learned that the women of Beaumont were not so naïve. He approached twenty three year old Terry Walden with his camera and an offer to do a free photo shoot, but was quickly rebuffed by the nursing student and mother of two.

Although Walden fit Wilder's victimology perfectly, as she was an attractive young woman, she was also known to her friends and family to be intelligent and street smart. She was attending Lamar to enhance her career prospects in order to provide a better home for her children; she was not there to become a model and would have been leery about such a proposal from a stranger.

But the sadistic impulses of the beauty queen killer were too much to control and so Wilder promptly moved his operations to the local mall.

Hunting at the local mall proved to be no better for Wilder as witnesses reported seeing him lurk around for hours, propositioning young women and girls with a free photo shoot. But Wilder was turned down time after time and when he appeared ready to give up and leave, fate intervened.

After Terry Walden's encounter with Christopher Wilder on the campus of Lamar University, she stopped by the local mall to pick up a few things before heading home. As Wilder was being shot down by another girl, he spied Walden's familiar face a few yards away. He approached Walden once more, attempted to strike up another conversation, and offered once more to take some free photos. Wilder must have believed that persistence pays off, but in this case he was sorely mistaken as once more, Walden soundly rejected his offer.

A trigger of rage went off inside Wilder as he watched Walden turn her back to him and walk out the mall's doors. How could this woman deny him? Who did she think she was?

The beauty queen killer would not be denied his sadistic pleasure – he had to kill Terry Walden.

In true hunter fashion, Wilder followed closely behind Walden, pouncing on her as she opened the door to her car. The beauty queen killer then pushed her into the car and drove her to a remote location where he raped, tortured, and then murdered the young mother. He then dumped her body in a canal, took her car, and left town.

When Walden did not return home, her family reported her missing. The FBI discovered her body on March 26 and Wilder's car in the mall parking lot. Hairs discovered in Wilder's abandoned vehicle were later determined to be those of Theresa Ferguson.

From Beaumont, Wilder drove north and caught Interstate 35 until he arrived in Oklahoma City, Oklahoma. After checking into a motel, Wilder drove to the Penn Square Mall to find his next victim on March 25. Wilder quickly learned that the young women and girls of Oklahoma City were a bit more naïve than the women of Beaumont. With camera in hand and business cards in his pocket, Wilder enticed twenty one year old Suzanne Logan to go with him on a photo shoot.

Once Logan sat in Wilder's car he threatened her with his gun and then, similar to the Grover assault, he drove across the state line to Newton, Kansas where he brought his victim to a motel room. Wilder spent the evening and part of the next day raping and brutalizing his helpless victim with crudely devised shocking devices he made from electrical cords.

After he was finished with Logan, he loaded her back into his car and drove north on Interstate 135 and then east on Interstate 70 until he reached the Junction City exit where he then drove a couple of miles north on U.S. Highway 77 to Milford Lake.

Suzanne Logan was physically diminished, but even worse, the young woman was mentally demoralized and unable to fight back, run, or even scream. She sat quietly in the car next to Wilder until they arrived at the lake. The beauty queen killer then led Logan out of the car and stabbed her to death on the shore of the lake.

The murder of Suzanne Logan represented another deviation of Wilder's normal M.O. – after abducting his victim, he took her to multiple locations before ultimately murdering her. Wilder may have been trying to throw the authorities off by moving his victim, or he could have taken Logan as a sexual slave and potential accomplice, as he did later in his murder spree. The exact reasons for Wilder's deviation from his standard M.O. will never be known, but it is known that after dumping Logan's body the beauty queen killer got on Interstate 70 and drove west.

Anyone who has driven across the Great Plains, especially on Interstate 70 across Kansas and eastern Colorado, knows what a desolate and lonely region it can be. Interstate exits are often far apart and outside of some grazing livestock, there is little to see. If one were to make the drive alone, as Wilder did, it would give a person a lot of time to think.

The solitude of the Great Plains is the type of place where a person can reexamine his life and decide where to go next, but for Wilder it appears that it only gave him the time to think of ways to perfect his M.O. and to think of more nefarious ways to torture his victims.

The beauty queen killer was not interested in introspection and self-reflection; he was only interested in sadism and murder, plain and simple.

After driving through the Rocky Mountains on Interstate 70, Wilder stopped in Rifle, Colorado and checked into a motel on March 29. From Rifle, the beauty queen killer then drove approximately another sixty miles west to the larger town of Grand Junction, Colorado. Grand Junction is not a particularly large city – its metropolitan area is around 150,000 people – but it is the largest population center in the area and most importantly for Wilder, there were malls and shopping centers.

Wilder quickly found the Mesa Mall in Grand Junction to be good hunting grounds as he was able to lure eighteen year old Sheryl Bonaventura into his car with promises of fame and fortune. Once in Wilder's car, Bonaventura quickly learned that she fell into the clutches of a sadist who proceeded to rape and torture her over the course of two days. Wilder's sadism was getting more extreme at this point; he was spending more time torturing his victims and he also started to experiment more with other forms of torture such as using electrical cords to shock and knives to leave several small, superficial but painful wounds.

Wilder may have been attempting to use Bonaventura as a prop to more easily lure other victims, as he did later in the spree with Tina Marie Risico, because witnesses claimed to have spotted Wilder, Bonaventura, and another young woman at a restaurant in Silverton, Colorado.

After what was probably at least two days of brutal torture, Bonaventura, like Logan days before, was a broken woman who could do little to resist her tormentor. As he ordered her back into the car she must have known what was coming next.

The beauty queen killer brought Bonaventura across state lines and then shot and stabbed her to death in rural Utah on March 31. It is unknown what happened to the other girl that was spotted with Wilder and Bonaventura; if true, the chances are good that she too was killed and dumped somewhere in the desert. There is also a good chance that the sighting was a red herring.

Christopher Bernard Wilder was becoming even more unhinged and it seems as though the FBI was powerless to stop him.

Wilder Stays One Step Ahead of the FBI's Technology

The FBI had their hands full in the hunt for Christopher Wilder because in many ways he was unlike any other spree and serial killer that they had encountered. Wilder was well funded, which meant that he would not have to rely on crimes such as burglary or armed robbery that could get him arrested sooner. Wilder also displayed above average intelligence, or at least an above average knowledge of law enforcement forensics and procedures in 1984.

But perhaps more importantly, Wilder had 1984 technology on his side.

In many ways the technology of 1984 was not drastically different than it is today: cell phones were available to those with money, although cell towers were few and far between, and home computers were becoming more and more popular. With that said, there were some noticeable differences that helped facilitate Wilder's flight from justice.

Although the predecessors of the internet as we know it today, such as ARPANET, were around in 1984, they were only available to a limited number of people, usually those working in the military and research. Email was also several years away from being a reality so the FBI and other law enforcement agencies were forced to communicate through telephone and teletype.

Before the internet, teletype was the standard way that news and law enforcement agencies instantly transmitted information to other agencies. For the most part, the teletype system was an efficient way to transmit important information, but it was far from being a webpage or message board where information can be posted and updated instantaneously. Teletype messages had to be read one at a time, which could severely hamper an investigation if there are a lot of tips.

"The FBI teletype system was backed up over forty eight hours for about two weeks because of the volume of information that was flowing back and forth on Wilder," stated Gordon McNeil on the problem.

But it was not only the technology available to law enforcement that hampered the hunt for Christopher Wilder; outdated credit card technology also helped the beauty queen killer evade capture.

Wilder used a combination of his own and some stolen credit cards to pay for motel rooms. Today, nearly every credit card purchase a person makes in the United States is instantly entered into the credit card company's database where the retailer at the point of purchase will be alerted if the card is stolen, maxed out, or sometimes if the holder is wanted by law enforcement. The FBI alerted all of Wilder's credit card companies about their manhunt, which responded by adding a note to Wilder's accounts on their computers that retailers should immediately call the police if spotted. The FBI also alerted all credit card companies that Wilder may be using a stolen credit card as he trekked west.

Unfortunately, many retailers in 1984 were still using non-computerized methods to complete credit card transactions, which further allowed Wilder to continue with his killing spree. Despite this, the FBI nearly caught up to Wilder in Rifle, Colorado where he used a stolen credit card to check into a motel room. Although the motel still used the "knuckle buster" method of recording credit card transactions, the front desk manager was suspicious and followed up with a call to the credit card company. The credit card company then alerted the FBI that its quarry may be in western Colorado, but by the time agents showed up Wilder was headed further west and Sheryl Bonaventura was dead.

It was as if the FBI had to wait for Wilder to kill again.

Getting More Brazen

The fact that the FBI was clearly on his tail did not slow down Wilder. In fact, it seems as if he relished the chase in some ways as the brutality of his crimes escalated along with a defiant attitude that seemed to challenge the FBI. The FBI plotted a potential course that Wilder was traveling and determined that he was headed to California and would probably pass through Las Vegas. Believing that they were ahead of Wilder, FBI agents canvassed nearly every mall between Salt Lake City and California with pictures of Wilder. If he showed up at a mall, the FBI would capture him.

But Wilder was still one step ahead of the Feds!

After killing Sheryl Bonaventura, Wilder continued west on Interstate 70 until the road terminates in the middle of rural Utah at Interstate 15, which he then followed southwest into Las Vegas. Las Vegas is aptly named "Sin City" because most of the vices known to man – sex, gambling, excessive food, and illicit drugs – are readily available and often legal. People from all over the world visit Las Vegas every day to party and gamble: it was a perfect place for Wilder to find his next victim and a good place to get lost in the crowd.

Although the FBI was hot on his tail and actively looking for him in shopping malls throughout the west, Wilder was undeterred and probably a bit thrilled with the "game." The beauty queen killer arrived in Las Vegas on April 1, tired and desperate to avoid capture. His desperation must have quickly turned to exhilaration when he learned that the teen magazine *Seventeen* was holding a modeling competition at the Meadows Mall.

Wilder showed no fear of law enforcement when he went to the competition, with his camera in hand, and sat directly front of the runway for all to see. Since there were numerous actual fashion photographers at the competition, a photo of Wilder was inadvertently taken. The picture shows Wilder eyeing his next victim, seventeen year old Michelle Korfman, with what was described as "the look of a homicidal maniac" by Gordon McNeil.

Out of all Wilder's victims, Michelle Korfman actually was an aspiring model. Tall, with stunning looks, Korfman had already competed in some smaller competitions before participating in the fateful Las Vegas competition. Korfman lived in suburban Boulder City, Nevada with her parents, so when she announced that she was picked to take part in the competition, she was allowed to travel there alone.

The beauty queen killer was waiting.

After the competition, Wilder approached the attractive girl with his standard line of a free portfolio to help her career. Korfman's guard was no doubt let down as photographers and fashion industry insiders were all over the mall and Wilder knew how to say the right words, which he no doubt perfected after numerous failures.

Evidence indicates that once Wilder successfully abducted Korfman, he raped and brutalized her in more than one location over the course of several days, as he did with his previous two victims. More than a month later, Michelle Korfman's body was found near a roadside rest stop in southern California. Korfman's body displayed much of the same brutality that Wilder employed on his previous victims, but she was also covered, from head to toes, with small incisions.

Wilder's increasing brutality and sadism was not lost on the FBI. McNeil noted that Wilder "was a brutal, sexual sadist" who became one of the FBI's top priorities. The FBI needed to act quickly.

Frustrated that the beauty queen killer continued to stay one step ahead of their technology and tactics, the FBI decided to play a new card from their deck: an appeal to the public through the media. On April 5, Gordon McNeil and other FBI agents on the Christopher Wilder taskforce held a press conference where they showed pictures of Wilder and discussed his M.O. The FBI also announced that Wilder had been added to the Top Ten list.

The FBI's Top Ten most wanted fugitive list began in 1950 and continues to the present. There is no particular order to the list; fugitives are merely grouped and classified together as the ten most wanted men, or women, in the United States. The list is routinely updated when fugitives are captured, learned to be deceased, or in Wilder's case, when a new, more dangerous fugitive arises. In 1984, which was a few years before television shows such as *America's Most Wanted* and *Unsolved Mysteries*, the Top Ten list was the primary tool that the FBI used to alert the public about dangerous fugitives. The list is displayed at post offices and other federal buildings and in an era before email when people routinely visited post offices, many people saw Wilder's picture.

The FBI was closing in on the beauty queen killer.

Tina Marie Risico

The FBI investigation of Christopher Bernard Wilder's 1984 cross-country killing spree followed a trajectory that was much different than other serial killer cases. In most serial killer cases, the police work frantically to identify the killer in order to stop the killings, but in the Wilder case the killer was known so it was just a matter of predicting where and when he would make his next move. The FBI tried to determine that based on his previous behavior, but serial killers, like most people, can act in unpredictable ways.

Shortly after disposing of Michelle Korfman, Wilder arrived in sunny southern California, which had at that time just recovered from a wave of violence at the hands of the "Hillside

Stranglers" Kenneth Bianchi and Angelo Buono, but had yet to be victimized by the "Nightstalker" Richard Ramirez.

Christopher Wilder was about to bring his brand of violence to the Los Angeles area.

As with most of his prior crimes, Wilder visited local malls looking for potential victims when he learned that the women of southern California, like those in Beaumont, Texas, were not so naïve.

The beauty queen killer set up shop in southern California at the Del Amo Fashion Center Mall in Torrance. Perhaps he thought that the name of the mall would help him find a victim more easily so he set about with his routine of approaching attractive young women and girls with his camera and business cards. The situation in Torrance began to be like Beaumont, although for different reasons.

Beaumont, Texas is a working-class city where the residents just do not have the time for get rich schemes and pipe dreams. The people of Beaumont are conservative and realistic so its residents were not as susceptible to Wilder's M.O. On the other hand, while there are a considerable number of blue collar people in southern California, it is also the home of Disneyland and Hollywood, where new people are discovered every day and dreams can come true. With that said, the average southern Californian is not naïve and hear get rich and "I'll make you famous" schemes every day. Many southern

Californians may dream of fame, but most know that the chances are remote that they will ever see it. They see people come to their state every day from around the world looking for fame so to many of them an Australian with a camera was just another person trying to live a Hollywood fantasy.

So when Wilder prowled the Del Amo Fashion Center Mall most were skeptical as they had heard it all before.

After being rejected by several women, Wilder met sixteen year old Tina Marie Risico. The beauty queen killer struck up a conversation with the attractive girl and learned that Risico was at the mall looking for a part-time job. She told Wilder that she was not interested in modeling, but the sadistic killer persisted. He offered her $100 to sweeten the deal, which made the cash strapped teenager relent.

Instead of turning on Risico immediately after the two got in the car, as he had done with most of his prior victims, Wilder brought the girl to a remote location for a photo shoot. According to Risico, the shoot began as planned, but after a few minutes Wilder pulled out his Python revolver and ordered her back into the car. Wilder then drove them south on Interstate 5 until they reached San Diego where he checked them into a motel.

The beauty queen killer then followed his standard pathology: he beat, raped, and tortured Risico over the course of several hours. When he was not raping Risico, Wilder was torturing the teenager by cutting her with a knife and shocking her with electrical cords.

Just when it appeared that Wilder was about to dispatch Risico as he had done to his prior victims, he stopped. Risico claims that Wilder had the television on during most of her ordeal in order to muffle the sounds of her screams so that other guests would not hear her, but stopped his torture when he heard his name mentioned – the FBI press conference was on the set. Wilder quickly gathered his things, including Risico, and fled the motel room, this time heading back east.

For some reason, the press conference alarmed Wilder. He knew that the FBI was after him so it is a bit surprising that seeing himself on the news had that much of an impact. But it was not just the April 5 FBI press conference, various media outlets – newspapers, magazines, and television – had all caught wind of the Wilder case and so began running the story. As Gordon McNeil noted: "It's the front page headline in every newspaper in America. Every news show, every radio show is talking about Christopher Wilder and showing his picture and saying his name – Christopher Wilder."

The hunter had become the hunted.

As Wilder drove out of San Diego east with Risico something incredible happened that will probably never be completely understood. Instead of killing the teenager and leaving her body on the side of a desolated highway in Arizona, he apparently formed a bond with her. The pair drove along Interstate 40 until it met Interstate 44 in Oklahoma City, which they then followed northeast to Saint Louis. Normally, such a drive would take at least twenty four hours, so chances are that the two either stopped at a motel or Risico did part of the driving.

From Saint Louis the pair then took Interstate 55 until it intersects Interstate 80, which they then took east until they reached Chicago's southeast suburbs across the state line into Indiana.

It was time for Wilder to find another victim and this time Risico would help him.

Most people have a difficult time trying to comprehend why a victim would help her attacker brutalize others. Because Risico helped Wilder capture two of his victims many people to this day believe she should have been charged as an accessory. One only has to do a cursory search of serial killer message boards that have threads dedicated to Christopher Wilder, as well as comment sections in more recent articles about the beauty queen killer, to see that Tina Marie Risico's involvement in the murder spree provokes a lot of anger and animosity.

The anger directed toward Risico is not totally fair though as she found herself in an unbelievably difficult situation that was not unique among the annals of criminal history.

The process in which Risico aided Wilder to claim his last victims is a professionally recognized psychological condition known as "Stockholm Syndrome." The condition is so-called after a 1973 bank robbery and standoff with the police in Stockholm, Sweden where hostages in the bank began to identify with the bank robbers. Numerous academic papers have been written on the subject and a number of hostage and kidnapping incidents have been identified, both before and after the 1973 Stockholm bank robbery, where hostages have shown signs of the syndrome. Furthermore, the FBI estimates that around 8% of hostages begin to identify with their abductors at some point.

On the other hand, some academics have identified another condition that has been termed the "Lima Syndrome" for a 1996 takeover of the Japanese embassy in Peru by leftist terrorists. In that case, the terrorists began to identify with hostages and eventually let several go, including one that proved to be a high value bargaining piece.

An examination of the Risico-Wilder relationship reveals that elements of the Stockholm and Lima syndrome were both at work. Through a combination of fear and desperation, Risico obediently followed Wilder's every order, while the beauty queen killer, perhaps showing a shred of humanity, eventually released his captive.

Those who criticize Risico also fail to take into consideration her age. Most sixteen year olds have few life experiences and no matter what one may learn in school or from parents, no one can say for sure what she would do if abducted by a sadistic serial killer. It was not like Risico signed up for Wilder's killing spree willingly; she was kidnapped, tortured, and raped like all of his other victims.

Truly, when Tina Marie Risico found herself in the clutches of the beauty queen killer she was in an impossible situation.

When the pair arrived in Merrillville, Indiana on April 10, they headed straight to the Southlake Mall so that Wilder could hunt for his next victim. But Wilder learned from his experiences in Texas and California that not every young woman and girl who frequent shopping malls are not as naïve as he would like.

He decided to change his M.O. a bit with Risico's help.

Wilder told Risico that he would release her if she helped him snatch a new victim from the mall. Risico was hesitant, but after a deranged combination of threats and praise, she eventually relented.

When they arrived at the mall, Wilder thought they could accomplish his goal quicker if they split up. Risico had a chance to either run or alert someone to her plight, but instead she helped capture Wilder's next victim, sixteen year old Dawnette Wilt.

Wilt and Risico had a number of things in common: they were both pretty sixteen year olds who liked to hang out in malls and on the fateful days that they both met Wilder they were also job hunting. Risico engaged Wilt in some average teenage small talk when she learned that Dawnette was at the mall looking for a part-time job. One can only wonder what went through Risico's mind when she heard that Wilder's next victim was at the mall for the same innocent reason that she was just a few days earlier; but whatever hesitation she may have had was quickly overcome when she told the hapless Wilt that her "boss", Wilder, was the manager of a store and looking for new employees. The two girls then found Wilder and the three left in Terry Walden's stolen car.

As soon as the three got into the car the situation turned once more. Wilder threatened Wilt's life, who then acquiesced to the killer's sadistic sexual demands. The beauty queen killer then followed his M.O. by leaving the area with both girls.

The three quietly drove east along Interstate 80 until it runs concurrent with Interstate 90 in Ohio and then followed Interstate 90 after the interstates diverged and continued on into western upstate New York.

Wilder then checked he and his two victims into a motel room where he raped and tortured Wilt, making Risico watch.

The psychological torture hit its peak at this point; Wilder now had two victims that he not only tortured physically, but he also forced one to be a participant, which no doubt added more emotional distress to Risico. It was too late for Tina Risico though, as she was completely beaten and under the control of Wilder – she would not fight back or try to run. The two girls would need a miracle if they were to survive.

Tina Marie Risico's disappearance did not go unnoticed by the FBI who quickly deduced, based on the circumstances as well as witness identification of Wilder at the Torrance mall, that the girl had been abducted by the beauty queen killer. The FBI appealed to the media once more by publishing photos of the sixteen year old and most importantly, allowing her mother to plead for her daughter's life on live television. On April 12, while Wilder was raping and torturing Wilt, Risico broke down in tears when she saw her mother on television beseeching the beauty queen killer to release her daughter.

Wilder also saw the news report and reacted the same way he did when he saw himself on the news on April 5 – he fled the motel in fear.

The beauty queen killer quickly loaded up the car and drove the two girls out to a rural location. It was time to clear up some more loose ends.

At gun point, Wilder forced Wilt out of the car and into a wooded area where he shot and stabbed the sixteen year old. He then walked back to the car, looked at Risico as if she was next, but then drove off down the road. As the two silently drove down the backroad to the main highway, Wilder suddenly turned the car around – he had to make sure Wilt was dead.

For some reason, despite strangling and stabbing Wilt numerous times, the beauty queen killer had a feeling that the girl survived his brutal attack. When he arrived at the location where he left Wilt, Wilder was surprised, scared, and angry that she was not there.

Did the police or some local residents already find her?

Wilder knew that it was just a matter of time, probably hours or less, until the FBI learned that he was in New York. It was time to keep moving.

As Dawnette Wilt lay bleeding and barely able to breathe, she summoned up enough strength to crawl from her intended grave. She crawled several yards until she thought she was far enough away to try to pull herself to her feet on the side of a tree. She tried a couple of times, but was unable to stay up due to blood loss. Dawn Wilt had to try something else.

Unable to muster enough energy to walk or even stand, Wilt summoned up all her strength and courage to crawl hundreds of yards until she made it to a major road. She then crawled along the shoulder of the road until some Good Samaritans stopped to help the beaten and battered teenager. Dawnette Wilt saved her life by crawling from the spot where Wilder left her not only because if she had stayed the beauty queen killer would have killed her when he returned, but also because if she would have tried walking to the road she would have probably have died from blood loss.

Local and federal authorities quickly learned that Wilt was just the latest victim in Christopher Wilder's cross-country killing spree and unfortunately she was not his last.

When he was unable to locate Wilt in the forest where he left her, Wilder jumped back into his car with Risico and head east down Interstate 90. He only drove as far as Victor, New York where he exited from the tollway and promptly found the Eastview Mall.

But this time Wilder was not looking for a young female victim, he was instead searching for a car to replace the stolen one he was driving. An APB of the car he was driving was sent to all law enforcement agencies across the country via teletype and although he frequently changed license plates, he knew that it was only a matter of time until he was pulled over.

When Wilder and Risico arrived at the Eastview Mall in Victor, it was a vastly different situation than the other mall visits the beauty queen killer made over the previous three weeks. Gone were his camera and business cards. He was not looking for a young attractive female to fulfill his twisted fantasies; he needed a clean car to escape the area.

Before the two began their hunt in the parking lot, Wilder briefed Risico on what he needed her to do. He told her that he would force a woman into her car and that Risico would then follow in Walden's car until they arrived at a remote location where they would then change cars.

If everything went according to plan, Wilder promised to release Risico.

It was not long before Wilder spied thirty three year old Elizabeth Dodge walking from the mall to her car. Although Dodge was an attractive woman, she was a bit out of Wilder's preferred age group, but the beauty queen killer was looking for a car, not fun.

Wilder crept up behind Dodge, put his Colt Python into her side, and ordered her into her car. As Wilder drove out of the parking lot in Dodge's firebird, Risico dutifully followed behind in Walden's automobile. Once the two cars had driven outside of town a few miles, Wilder pulled over in a remote location, ordered Dodge out of the car, and then unceremoniously shot her to death.

The beauty queen killer then ordered Risico into Dodge's car and the two continued their eastward journey down Interstate 90. The two drove silently through the night; there were no road trip games such as name the license plate, only silence. In the early morning hours the two arrived at Interstate 90's eastern terminus at Boston's Logan International Airport. Wilder then went into the airport and bought a one way ticket to Los Angeles for Risico.

The worst part of Tina Marie Risico's nightmare was over. She and Wilt both somehow survived the clutches of the beauty queen killer.

After she arrived home, Risico was debriefed by the FBI and then went into obscurity, changing her identity in order to avoid the media and potentially violent vigilantes who blamed her for the assault on Wilt and the murder of Dodge.

The beauty queen killer would not take another female's life, but he still had two more victims to claim.

Heading North

From Logan International Airport, Wilder got back onto the freeway system and headed north on Interstate 95. It was believed that he was headed north to enter Canada in an effort to avoid capture.

Wilder's flight north to Canada presents another interesting aspect of the beauty queen killer case that displays more of his myopic and somewhat illogical thinking. Although Wilder had friends and business associates in Canada, none were involved in criminal activity so there is little reason to believe that any would have helped him avoid arrest. Also, crossing the border would not have lessened the law enforcement hunt because the two countries have an extradition agreement.

"During the search for Wilder we knew that he had friends in Canada and had visited Canada extensively," said Gordon

McNeil on Wilder's flight north. "So we felt there was a good chance that he was heading directly east and then north into Canada."

Apparently though, Wilder's sadistic urges were too much for him to quell on the day long drive from Boston to Canada, so he pulled over in Beverly, Massachusetts to find a new victim.

At the end of his murder spree it appears that Wilder had grown sloppy, desperate or a combination of both because he tried to abduct nineteen year old Carol Hilbert from a parking lot in Beverly. In his previous successful abductions, Wilder took his time in order to effectively use his photographer ruse, but this abduction was rushed and the intended victim saw him coming.

Not only was the kidnapping unsuccessful, but he was spotted by witnesses who gave the police a description of the attacker and his car.

The FBI now knew that Wilder was in Massachusetts headed north and they also knew the car he was driving. The beauty queen killer's days were numbered.

After the assault in Beverly, Wilder then took Interstate 93 north into New Hampshire and then got on U.S. Highway 3, which crosses into Canada near the town of Colebrook.

Crossing the U.S.-Canadian border in 1984 was quite a bit different than it is today. In 1984, travelers only needed to show a legitimate driver's license to cross either side and at some of the less traveled crossings people were even allowed to cross sometimes with no identification. For the most part, the identification checks at the border crossings in 1984 were a formality as only the largest crossings had available computer databases to check for fugitives and there were not yet laws on the books that prevented convicted felons from crossing into either country. With that said, Wilder's picture was posted at nearly every border crossing as all agents from both sides of the border were ordered to be on the lookout for the sadistic killer.

But Wilder was still one step ahead of the authorities. Perhaps he could get lucky – he had been lucky before!

The beauty queen killer eyed the border near Colebrook with trepidation. He knew that if they recognized him it was over, so there was no use using his driver's license. After driving around Colebrook for a while, Wilder stopped at a gas station to fill up before he attempted to cross the border. The beauty queen killer took his time at the gas station by washing the windows on Dodge's car and then engaging the store attendants in small talk. The focus of Wilder's conversation was the border: how many agents man it and what type of paperwork would he need to cross. In particular, he asked if he could cross over with an identification other than a driver's license.

Leo Jellison and Wayne Fortier were two New Hampshire state troopers doing a daily patrol near the border. The two troopers were aware of the Christopher Wilder manhunt, but neither thought the sadistic serial killer would up anywhere near Colebrook, New Hampshire.

Elizabeth Dodge's stolen car is what the two troopers noticed first.

The New Hampshire state police had briefed its officers a number of times on the Wilder case and most importantly, had updated them on the Elizabeth Dodge murder and were warned to be on the lookout for her stolen car.

They called in the sighting with the dispatch and confirmed that the car was Dodge's.

The New Hampshire state police had cornered the beauty queen killer!

Wilder noticed the two troopers across the street, but he continued his conversation with the attendants, hoping that they would keep going.

As soon as the troopers walked into the parking lot Wilder ran for his car. Trooper Jellison then grabbed Wilder from behind and the two struggled for the beauty queen killer's Colt Python. Wilder won the struggle, but instead of turning to shoot the trooper, he shot himself in the heart. The bullet went through Wilder's body, killing him instantly, and into the trooper. Trooper Jellison recovered from the wound and later returned to duty with a scar to remind him and others of how he stopped the nightmare of the beauty queen killer.

Just like that, as quickly as Christopher Bernard Wilder's killing spree began, it ended.

CHAPTER 5:
Final Considerations

For most serial killers, their capture only represents the end of one chapter in their lives. Many spend long lives in prison giving numerous interviews to journalists and scholars who try to understand their motives. Some become the focus of affection for deranged serial killer fans and some, such as the "Night Stalker" Richard Ramirez, even wed behind bars. Even serial killers sentenced to death usually spend several years, or even decades, on death row, so there are plenty of chances for the killer to tell his story to the public.

This was obviously not the case with Christopher Bernard Wilder.

Wilder's sudden death in New Hampshire combined with the fact that he left behind no writings that detail his crimes has left a lot of unanswered questions about the case. His known friends and business associates all claim that they never would have imagined Wilder embarking on a cross-country killing spree and that he never intimated a desire to do such a thing.

Wilder's death brought to surface some immediate questions that are still unanswered: what drove the beauty queen killer to kill, was he an actual serial killer, and were there other victims?

What Drove the Beauty Queen Killer?

Determining how a person thinks is a tricky and sometimes impossible venture, especially when abnormal behavior is involved. Psychiatrists can determine if someone's brain has suffered physical damage, but problems with the personality are not so easy to identify.

Brain damage has been pointed to by some scholars as a possible cause for the homicidal urge of many serial killers. Studies have been done on the brains of serial killers with some reports indicating that many serial killer had damage to their frontal lobes, but the evidence remains inconclusive and in Wilder's case, not applicable. After Wilder's death, he was cremated in Florida, although a person reportedly called the New Hampshire pathologist who conducted the autopsy on the beauty queen killer in an effort to obtain his brain.

With that said, the problems with his birth and his near drowning death a few years later may have left brain damage and the electro-shock therapy has also been considered as a contributing factor to Wilder's homicidal impulses. The reality is that biological reasons for Wilder's killing spree will probably never be known so it may be more productive to look for other reasons.

A lack of finances and/or debt has been the cause of numerous crimes throughout history. Extreme cases of debt have been the apparent cause of some people to kill, even their own families. Straight laced banker John List killed his entire family in 1971 and then assumed a new identity to escape debt. Even some well-known serial killers, such as Donald Gaskins, were driven at least partially by greed as he was worked part-time as a hitman and killed people who owed him money.

But Christopher Bernard Wilder was worth $2 million upon his death.

In fact, an examination of Wilder reveals that in many ways he lived a charmed life: he had plenty of money and material possessions, was respected by his neighbors and colleagues, and was popular with women.

If there were no financial reasons for Wilder to kill and if no one can say for sure if he had physical damage to his brain, then the possibility of a psycho-sexual disorder remains.

Wilder shared a similar psychological trait with most other serial killers, no matter their backgrounds – he lacked empathy. The beauty queen killer's lack of empathy for other humans was closely tied to his extreme ego and feeling of grandiosity; Wilder believed that he was God's gift to women and that they were merely there to pleasure him.

People who knew Wilder said that he like to throw parties at his house and show off his cars and boats to his friends. Although he was described as always being a good host, he no doubt did so to appease his own ego and sense of superiority. It gave Wilder a sense of power to have other wealthy people visit his home so that he could show them how well he had done and that he belonged among their ranks.

Some experts have pointed out that Wilder's grandiosity and megalomania led him to snap when Elizabeth Kenyon refused his marriage proposal, which may explain her murder but not the others after, or all the sexual assaults he committed prior.

Wilder clearly suffered from sexual problems as he had an unhealthy view of women and sexuality in general. Obviously, as detailed in this book, Wilder's sexual deviancy began at a young age and only progressed as the years went on so the murders can be seen as the logical culmination in the twisted career of a sexual sadist. The extreme types of torture he inflicted on his victims and the fact that he often masturbated before raping the women indicates that Wilder's sexual deviancy was deep seated probably began during his childhood, as it does for most adult sex offenders.

There are no records of Christopher Wilder ever being sexually assaulted as a child in Australia and all of his surviving family members have remained tight lipped about anything having to do with his life so the world will probably never know what made Wilder a sexual sadist and what ultimately drove him to start killing in the spring of 1984.

It could just be that Wilder was born evil.

Ultimately, questions concerning Christopher Wilder's murderous motives are quickly replaced with more important questions such as: can he even be considered a true serial killer?

The term "serial killer" was first coined by the FBI in the late 1970s to define someone who has killed three or more people in a series, with a significant "cooling off" period at some point between kills. The motives can be diverse – profit, political, sexual gratification, thrill – and often the killer is driven by a combination of desires. The victimology, pathology, and M.O. of the killer are not important, although they help investigators place potential serial killers into sub-categories for study. So then, based on the most basic definition of the term serial killer, did Christopher Wilder meet the standard?

Although Wilder killed more than three people in a series, there is debate as to whether there was the required "cool down" period between victims. There were of course days between the murders of some of his victims, but those were usually when he was traveling to his next location and as his spree progressed, he usually had a victim in tow.

Wilder's cross-country odyssey of murder closely matches that of Charles Starkweather, who murdered eleven people across the states of Nebraska and Wyoming in late 1957 and early 1958. Starkweather, like Wilder, killed different people he met during his crime spree for money and cars, but was not a sexual sadist. He tried to unsuccessfully rape one of his female victims before killing her and seemed to pick his victims much more randomly than Wilder. Charles Starkweather also had a female accomplice, Caril Ann Fugate, and had a classic "cool down" period between his first and second murders of two months. Despite meeting some of the basic criteria, Starkweather is not considered a serial killer by most experts.

The beauty queen killer case also shares some similarities with the 1997 Andrew Cunanan murder spree. Cunanan's spree lasted from April until July, covered several states, and left five men dead. The Cunanan case was different though in that sexual deviancy does not to appear to have been part of his M.O. The background of his victims was also quite varied as some were acquaintances, others were strangers, and one, Gianni Versace, was a celebrity.

Also, Wilder, Starkweather, and Cunanan all took their secrets to the grave.

Experts are divided over whether Starkweather and Cunanan can be defined as serial killers because the required "cool down" period is not apparent in either of their killing careers, so they are often termed "spree killers."

Wilder then may go down in the annals of criminal history as a spree, not a serial killer, unless other murders can be linked to him.

Other Potential Victims

The cold, hard reality is that someone as sadistic as Wilder, who showed a propensity for sexual violence at a young age, probably killed more than the nine women during his 1984 murder spree. In the years subsequent to Wilder's death, authorities in both the United States and Australia have looked at the beauty queen killer as a suspect in a number of cold cases. In some cases the M.O. closely matches Wilder's, while in others the beauty queen killer was known to be in the area.

Unfortunately, in many of the cold cases where Wilder is a suspect, the physical evidence has been degraded, witnesses are now dead, and/or a body has never been recovered so authorities do not even know if they have a murder on their hands.

The Wanda Beach Slayings

On January 12, 1965 the people of Sydney, Australia were shocked to learn that the mutilated bodies of two local girls were discovered on Wanda Beach. Wanda Beach was a popular recreation destination for the residents of Sydney who to this day swim, surf, and sunbathe on the beach located just outside of Australia's largest city. The two victims were fifteen year olds Marianne Schmidt and Christine Sharrock.

The two girls went down to the beach on January 11 to enjoy the wonderful summer weather of the southern hemisphere when what police believe was a single individual sexually assaulted and then murdered both girls. The girls were bound with duct tape, stabbed several times and left in a shallow grave. Sharrock also suffered a blow to the head. Strangely, although traces of semen were found on both girls, an autopsy revealed that neither had been penetrated.

The last witness to see the girls alive saw them walking quickly up the beach being followed by a young man.

The Wanda Beach slayings became front page headline fodder in a country that had relatively low crime rates at the time and brutal double homicides were almost unheard of. The public grew increasingly upset by the case when the local police failed to arrest anyone or even to produce a suspect.

In the decades since the Wanda Beach murders, the authorities developed a number of reasonable suspects and at the top of the list is Christopher Bernard Wilder.

Wilder became a suspect in the Wanda Beach slayings for a number of reasons. To begin with, Sydney was Wilder's hometown and he was known to not only frequent the area beaches, but he was arrested for his role in a gang-rape at an area beach in 1963. The M.O. in the gang-rape and the Wanda Beach case is obviously quite different; Wilder worked with a group during the 1963 assault while authorities believe the Wanda Beach killer worked alone.

But there are too many other similarities that cannot be ignored.

Both victims in the Wanda Beach murders were attractive and young – fifteen was a common age for many of Wilder's sexual assault and murder victims. It also seems that the two girls were somehow lured away from the main beach to a more isolated area where they were then sexually assaulted and murdered, which follows Wilder's M.O. beginning in the early 1970s in Florida.

Wilder also stabbed many of his victims to death in 1984, similar to the Wanda Beach murders, and perhaps most telling but overlooked is the fact that although semen was found on the victims, neither was penetrated. Based on the accounts of the survivors of Wilder's 1984 spree, the beauty queen killer often manually stimulated himself and sometimes reached climax before raping his victims.

The semen sample and blood that was identified as belonging to a male found on one of the girls is too small and degraded to produce any viable information so at this point the police are at an impasse in the investigation, but believe the killings may be related to two more that happened just over a year later.

In January and February of 1966, two women were strangled and stabbed to death on the streets of Sydney. The Sydney police have said that they believe the two cases are related and that those murders are related to the Wanda Beach slayings, although they have yet to say why they believe so.

The real possibility exists that Christopher Bernard Wilder began his serial killer career in Australia long before in 1984 spree, but other evidence also suggests that he may have left many more victims throughout the lakes, canals, and swamps of Florida.

More Possible Victims in Florida

If Wilder committed the Wanda Beach murders and the two killings one year later in Sydney, then he would truly be a serial killer by any definition as he had a significant time to "cool off" until his 1984 killing spree.

But was that too much time for someone like the beauty queen killer to cool off?

It would seem that once someone like Wilder began killing that he would not wait so long to kill again. This does not mean that Wilder did not commit the Wanda Beach murders only that more possible victims exist. Presently, Australian authorities have not publicly announced that Wilder is a suspect in any other unsolved murders in that country so one must look to Florida for more possible victims.

Since Florida became a state in 1845, it has attracted millions of people from around the world who have come to enjoy the state's warm weather, beaches, and attractions such as Disney World. Along with the vacationing families and retirees from the northeast, a number of infamous killers, such as Christopher Wilder, have also made the Sunshine State their home, which makes attributing cold cases to the beauty queen killer difficult. Many drifters have traveled through and committed crimes in Florida while Wilder lived there and a number of serial killers, such as Henry Lucas and Ottis Toole, operated right in the beauty queen killer's backyard during the 1970s and '80s.

With that said, the FBI and local Florida authorities have narrowed down five murders that Christopher Wilder may have committed.

Fort Meyers, Florida and Miami are only separated by 152 miles, which only takes about two and a half hours to travel on the section of Interstate 75 known as "alligator alley." Wilder was known to have business in the Fort Meyers area and visited the city frequently in the early 1980s, which is one of the reasons why he is a suspect in the murders of eighteen year old Mary Hare and seventeen year old Mary Opitz.

Opitz was an attractive brunette who was not known to have any problems in school or to be involved in drug or other criminal activity. She vanished from the parking lot of the Edison Mall on January 16, 1981. Her body has never been found and her case is still officially listed as a missing person. Wilder's proximity and M.O. of hunting in shopping malls makes him sound like a good suspect for Opitz's kidnapping and murder, which is magnified when another kidnapping and murder from the same location is considered.

Mary Hare, like Mary Opitz, was an attractive brunette who was last seen in the parking lot of the Edison Mall in Fort Myers. Hare was a waitress at a local restaurant and like Opitz, had no enemies. The young waitress was abducted a month after Opitz on February 16, but Hare's body was discovered several months later, severely decomposed, in a rural area. Despite the state of decomposition, forensic investigators were able to determine that Hare suffered several stab wounds.

Both Opitz and Hare were attractive girls, disappeared from shopping malls, and were squarely in the age range of Wilder's preferred victims.

In 1982 the skeletal remains of two females were discovered in a rural area of southeastern Florida near some property that Wilder owned. Neither of the two women has been identified and one of the women had her fingers removed, which authorities believe points to her knowing her killer. The two women had no doubt met early deaths through foul play, but due to the advanced stage of decomposition, forensic examiners could only determine that one victim had been dead for several years and the other for several months to two years.

Shari Lynn Ball was a twenty year old aspiring model who disappeared in June 1983 from her Boca Raton, Florida home. Ball last spoke with her mother on June 27, 1983, when she told her that she was moving to New York to pursue an acting career. Shari then told her mother that she was meeting a friend in Boynton Beach who would join her on the trip. Ball's mother's boyfriend claimed to have spoken with Shari a couple of days later on the phone, who told him that she was fine and at a truck stop in Virginia.

Shari Ball was never heard from again.

Her body was discovered in upstate New York a few months later, but not positively identified until 2014. The location of Ball's body may seem a little outside of Wilder's geographic comfort zone for 1983, but he was known to travel a lot to the north and Boynton Beach was his primary hunting ground. He could have snatched Ball with one of his typical ruses and then brought her north as he attended to other business and then disposed of her.

Wilder was also a person of interest in the disappearance of eighteen year old Tammy Lynn Leppert on July 6, 1983.

Leppert was a teenage beauty queen who had competed in hundreds of pageants and had begun working as an actor at the time of her disappearance. The beautiful young woman had a photogenic personality and looks that could have brought her far in either modeling or acting. Leppert disappeared from the convenience store she worked at in Merritt Island, Florida, which also happened to be the same city where Wilder abducted and murdered Theresa Ferguson.

On the night she vanished, Leppert got into an argument with a male friend of hers, who claims he dropped her off in a parking lot. Authorities had no real leads when Christopher Wilder's name surfaced in reference to the numerous sexual assaults he committed in the 1970s and early 1980s. Leppert's family pressed the authorities to arrest Wilder, but since there was no body and DNA evidence was not yet a reality in 1983, no arrest was made. Eventually, the Leppert family took the case into their own hands and filed a civil lawsuit against Wilder, but dropped the suit after he died, citing that they no longer believed the beauty queen killer to be Tammy's murderer.

The body of a young woman, now known as Broward County Jane Doe, was retrieved from a canal just to the north of Miami in Davie, Florida. The body was discovered on February 18, 1984, but was believed to have been in the canal for at least a couple of days before it was discovered due to its decomposition. The Broward County Jane Doe, who was strangled to death, had blonde hair and blue eyes and was probably in her twenties. If Wilder murdered this young woman, then it would have been the first in his spree. Until the woman is positively identified, authorities will be left guessing if she was truly one of the beauty queen killer's victims.

There is also a strong possibility that Wilder is responsible for the kidnapping and murder of nineteen year old Melody Gay. Gay was abducted while working the graveyard shift at a Collier County, Florida convenience store on March 7, 1984, two days after Wilder killed Elizabeth Kenyon. Gay's body was discovered on March 10 floating in a canal. Wilder would have had more than enough time to have killed Gay between Kenyon and Orsborne, in fact he would have had time to kill other women as well.

Finally, there is a Jane Doe discovered in San Francisco in 1984 who some authorities believe to be one of Wilder's west coast victims. Those who argue against Wilder's role in the Jane Doe's murder state that it would have been difficult for him to be in a San Diego motel room with Risico on April 5 and then travel north hundreds of miles to San Francisco to murder the Jane Doe and make it to suburban Chicago by April 10. Actually, five days is plenty of time to make that trip along Interstate 80, although the one living witness of the road trip,

Tina Marie Risico, stated that they took a different route to the Midwest.

The chances are remote that Wilder killed all of these potential victims; but when one considers the victimology and M.O., the chances are extremely high that he killed at least one and likely that he is responsible for multiple unsolved homicides.

The world may never know the exact number of women that fell into the sadistic clutches of Christopher Wilder, but the number of lives he destroyed was immense and continues to be felt today through the family members of the women he killed and assaulted.

The Collector

One of the more interesting, but little discussed, aspects of the Christopher Wilder case is his fascination with the 1963 John Fowles novel *The Collector*. The novel is about a socially awkward butterfly collector who becomes fixated on a young woman. After admiring the young woman from afar and then stalking her, the novel's protagonist then kidnaps the woman and adds her to his collection.

Although the protagonist never raped or beat his victim, she eventually dies due to an illness, which leaves the collector upset. The collector's sadness soon passes when he finds his victim's diary and learns that she never loved him; he then makes plans to kidnap another woman.

The novel was found with Wilder's other possessions when authorities searched Dodge's stolen car and witnesses claim that he loved the book so much that he memorized it. Wilder's fondness for *The Collector* is not unique among his fellow serial killers and presents an interesting story in itself.

During the early 1980s, Leonard Lake and Charles Ng murdered up to twenty five people at their mountain compound in northern California. The duo murdered men, women, and children, but the women were often kept alive for days or weeks for the two to torture and rape before they would kill them. Lake, who was the brains behind the sadistic operation, stated on video tape that his intent was to capture women to act as his sexual and domestic slaves. He also mentioned his fondness for *The Collector* and even named his killing spree "Operation Miranda" after the novel's female victim.

A few months after Wilder was killed, Robert Berdella embarked on his own spree of rape, torture, and murder in the Kansas City area. Unlike Wilder, Berdella's victims were all men, but they were young, attractive, and lured to their death under false pretenses, which was a similar M.O. to the beauty queen killer. Berdella also tortured his victims for days or even weeks with electrical cords and even blinded one of his victims, much like Wilder tried to do to Linda Grover.

Robert Berdella was also a fan of *The Collector*!

No one will say that *The Collector* made Wilder, Lake, or Berdella kill, but it is interesting and possibly even important when one considers that all three were especially sadistic sexual killers who used some of the same methods. Understanding the book and its protagonist may help in better understanding the motivations of sexual sadists.

Conclusion

The story of Christopher Bernard Wilder is a complex one where a seemingly normal and likeable person hid deep and dangerous secrets and desires from all of those around him. Wilder functioned and acted not only as a normal person for the majority of his life, but in his adulthood as a respected and important member of his local community. He was a man that many people looked up to and trusted.

He was reasonably intelligent and attractive and had attained financial and professional success by the time of his death. He could engage anyone in a conversation, which unfortunately led to the death of at least nine women and several more assaulted.

But Wilder's success and even his personality were just part of a façade he had built to cover his true sadistic nature.

"I think an important point to make is that these people are not always demons and they're not, they don't always have tattoos and long hair," commented surviving Wilder victim Linda Grover on the beauty queen killer's smooth persona. "They're often extremely eloquent and they're disguised and they can come into your father's living room after dinner sipping a wine or a brandy."

Wilder consciously developed his façade in order to mask the growing sexual sadism that he could not control as he reached adulthood in the 1970s and '80s and as he became a more sophisticated criminal, he learned how to use the two in tandem. The beauty queen killer learned how to use his charm in order for his victims to let their guards down.

After that the rest was history.

Despite Wilder's uncanny ability to get others to let their guards down in his presence, there were numerous warning signs before the 1984 murder spree.

Wilder's numerous arrests in both Australia and the United States should have been a warning sign to authorities in the two countries that he had serious problems that needed to be addressed. Perhaps that is the biggest tragedy of the Christopher Wilder case – the inaction by authorities to act when they were clearly faced with a disturbed person.

With that said, there was probably little that the authorities could have done at the time due to the much more lax sentencing guidelines in both countries.

So would current laws have stopped Wilder from killing as many women as he did?

This is a difficult question to answer, but one that is worth considering. To begin with, he would have served some significant time in an Australian prison for his role in the 1963 gang-rape. If he would have gone to the United States after serving time for that crime, then the numerous sex crimes he committed throughout the 1970s would probably have been treated more severely. His ability to abscond from his 1982 sexual assault charges in Australia would also have been curtailed due to current database technology employed at international airports in Australia and the United States.

The current laws in both Australia and the United States may have put him in prison, but there is no guarantee that he would not have embarked on a killing spree at another point in time in the United States, or in Australia.

The reality is that Christopher Bernard Wilder was not like the vast majority of humans. Wilder was the epitome of a sexual sadist; he found enjoyment and sexual gratification by hurting and killing women and the evidence shows that he felt that way for most of his life.

Whether Christopher Wilder was born a sexual sadist or became one through a trauma he suffered as a child is not important because the evidence shows that those unnatural urges overwhelmed him for most of his life.

The only way that the beauty queen killer could have been stopped was by locking him in prison for ever, or by giving him an early grave as he did to himself.

The main book has ended, but keep turning the pages and you will find some more information as well as some free content that I've added for you!

GET ONE OF MY AUDIOBOOKS FOR FREE

audible
an amazon company

If you haven't joined Audible yet, you can get any of my audiobooks for FREE!
Click on the image or <u>HERE</u> and click "Buy With Audible Credit" and you will get the audiobook for FREE!

More books by Jack Rosewood

Among the annals of American serial killers, few were as complex and prolific as Joseph Paul Franklin. At a gangly 5'11, Franklin hardly looked imposing, but once he put a rifle in his hands and an interracial couple in his cross hairs, Joseph Paul Franklin was as deadly as any serial killer. In this true crime story you will learn about how one man turned his hatred into a vocation of murder, which eventually left over twenty people dead across America. Truly, Franklin's story is not only that of a true crime serial killer, but also one of racism in America as he chose Jews, blacks, and especially interracial couples as his victims.

Joseph Paul Franklin's story is unique among serial killers biographies because he gained no sexual satisfaction from his murders and there is no indication that he was ever compelled to kill. But make no mistake about it, by all definitions; Joseph Paul Franklin was a serial killer. In fact, the FBI stated that Franklin was the first known racially motivated serial killer in the United States: he planned to kill as many of his perceived enemies as possible in order to start an epic race war across the country. An examination of Franklin's life will reveal how he became a racially motivated serial killer and the steps he took to carry out his one man war against the world.

Open the pages of this e-book to read a disturbing story of true crime murder in America's heartland. You will be disturbed and perplexed at Franklin's murderous campaign as he made himself a one man death squad, eliminating as many of his political enemies that he could. But you will also be captivated with Franklin's shrewdness and cunning as he avoided the authorities for years while he carried out his diabolical plot!

When Chris Bryson was discovered nude and severely beaten stumbling down Charlotte Street in Kansas City in 1988, Police had no idea they were about to discover the den of one of the most sadistic American serial killers in recent history. This is the true historical story of Robert Berdella, nicknamed by the media the Kansas City Butcher, who from between 1984 and 1988 brutally raped, tortured and ultimately dismembered 6 young male prostitutes in his unassuming home on a quiet street in Kansas City.

Based on the actual 720 page detailed confession provided by Berdella to investigators, it represents one of the most gruesome true crime stories of all time and is unique in the fact that it details each grizzly murder as told by the killer himself. From how he captured each man, to the terrifying methods he used in his torture chamber, to ultimately how he disposed of their corpses - rarely has there ever been a case where a convicted serial killer confessed to police in his own words his crimes in such disturbing detail.

Horrific, shocking and rarely equaled in the realms of sadistic torture – Berdella was a sexually driven lust killer and one of the most sadistic sex criminals ever captured. Not for the faint of heart, this is the tale of Robert "Bob" Berdella, the worst serial killer in Kansas City History and for those that are fans of historical serial killers, is a true must read.

Richmond, Virginia: On the morning of October 19, 1979, parolee James Briley stood before a judge and vowed to quit the criminal life. That same day, James met with brothers Linwood, Anthony, and 16-year-old neighbor Duncan Meekins. What they planned—and carried out—would make them American serial-killer legends, and reveal to police investigators a 7-month rampage of rape, robbery, and murder exceeding in brutality already documented cases of psychopaths, sociopaths, and sex criminals.

As reported in this book, the Briley gang were responsible for the killing of 11 people (among these, a 5-year-old boy and his pregnant mother), but possibly as many as 20. Unlike most criminals, however, the Briley gang's break-ins and robberies were purely incidental—mere excuses for rape and vicious thrill-kills. When authorities (aided by plea-bargaining Duncan Meekins) discovered the whole truth, even their tough skins crawled. Nothing in Virginian history approached the depravities, many of which were committed within miles of the Briley home, where single father James Sr. padlocked himself into his bedroom every night.

But this true crime story did not end with the arrests and murder convictions of the Briley gang. Linwood, younger brother James, and 6 other Mecklenburg death-row inmates, hatched an incredible plan of trickery and manipulation—and escaped from the "state-of-the-art" facility on May 31, 1984. The biggest death-row break-out in American history.

During fifty one days in early 1993 one of the most tragic events in American crime history unfolded on the plains outside Waco, Texas. An obscure and heavily armed religious sect called the Branch Davidians was barricaded inside their commune and outside were hundreds of law enforcement angry because the former had killed four ATF agents in a botched raid. Open the pages of this book and go on an engaging and captivating ride to examine one of the most important true crime stories in recent decades. Read the shocking true story of how a man the government considered a psychopath, but whose followers believed to be a prophet, led a breakaway sect of the Seventh Day Adventist Church into infamy.

You will follow the meteoric rise of the Branch Davidians' charismatic leader, David Koresh, as he went from an awkward kid in remedial classes to one of the most infamous cult leaders in world history. But the story of the Waco Siege begins long before the events of 1993. At the core of the conflict between the Branch Davidians and the United States government were ideas and interpretations of religious freedom and gun ownership, which as will be revealed in the pages of this book, a considerable philosophical gulf existed between the two sides. David Koresh and the Branch Davidians carried on a long tradition in American and Texas history of religious dissent, but in 1993 that dissent turned tragically violent.

You will find that beyond the standard media portrayals of the Waco Siege was an event comprised of complex human characters on both sides of the firing line and that perhaps the most tragic aspect of the event was that the extreme bloodshed could have been avoided.

The pages of this book will make you angry, sad, and bewildered; but no matter the emotions evoke, you will be truly moved by the events of the Waco Siege.

GET THESE BOOKS FOR FREE

Go to www.jackrosewood.com

and get these E-Books for free!

A Note From The Author

Hello, this is Jack Rosewood. Thank you for reading Christopher Wilder: The True Story of The Beauty Queen Killer. I hope you enjoyed the read of this chilling story. If you did, I'd appreciate if you would take a few moments to post a review on Amazon.

I would also love if you'd sign up to my newsletter to receive updates on new releases, promotions and a FREE copy of my Herbert Mullin E-Book, go to www.JackRosewood.com

Best Regards
Jack Rosewood

FREE BONUS CHAPTER

The making of a serial killer

"I was born with the devil in me," said H.H. Holmes, who in 1893 took advantage of the World's Fair – and the extra room he rented out in his Chicago mansion – to kill at least 27 people without attracting much attention.

"I could not help the fact that I was a murderer, no more than the poet can help the inspiration to sing. I was born with the evil one standing as my sponsor beside the bed where I was ushered into the world, and he has been with me since," Holmes said.

The idea of "I can't help it" is one of the hallmarks of many serial killers, along with an unwillingness to accept responsibility for their actions and a refusal to acknowledge that they themselves used free will to do their dreadful deeds.

"Yes, I did it, but I'm a sick man and can't be judged by the standards of other men," said Juan Corona, who killed 25 migrant workers in California in the late 1960s and early 1970s, burying them in the very fruit orchards where they'd hoped to build a better life for their families.

Dennis Rader, who called himself the BTK Killer (Bind, Torture, Kill) also blamed some unknown facet to his personality, something he called Factor X, for his casual ability to kill one family, then go home to his own, where he was a devoted family man.

"When this monster entered my brain, I will never know, but it is here to stay. How does one cure himself? I can't stop it, the monster goes on, and hurts me as well as society. Maybe you can stop him. I can't," said Rader, who said he realized he was different than the other kids before he entered high school. "I actually think I may be possessed with demons."

But again, he blamed others for not stopping him from making his first murderous move.

"You know, at some point in time, someone should have picked something up from me and identified it," he later said.

Rader was not the only serial killer to place the blame far away from himself.

William Bonin actually took offense when a judge called him "sadistic and guilty of monstrous criminal conduct."

"I don't think he had any right to say that to me," Bonin later whined. "I couldn't help myself. It's not my fault I killed those boys."

It leaves us always asking why

For those of us who are not serial killers, the questions of why and how almost always come to mind, so ill equipped are we to understand the concept of murder on such a vast scale.

"Some nights I'd lie awake asking myself, 'Who the hell is this BTK?'" said FBI profiler John Douglas, who worked the Behavioral Science Unit at Quantico before writing several best-selling books, including "Mindhunter: Inside the FBI's Elite Serial Crime Unit," and "Obsession: The FBI's Legendary Profiler Probes the Psyches of Killers, Rapists, and Stalkers and Their Victims and Tells How to Fight Back."

The questions were never far from his mind - "What makes a guy like this do what he does? What makes him tick?" – and it's the kind of thing that keeps profilers and police up at night, worrying, wondering and waiting for answers that are not always so easily forthcoming.

Another leader into the study of madmen, the late FBI profiler Robert Ressler - who coined the terms serial killer as well as criminal profiling – also spent sleepless nights trying to piece together a portrait of many a killer, something that psychiatrist James Brussel did almost unfailingly well in 1940, when a pipe bomb killer enraged at Con Edison was terrorizing New York City.

(Brussel told police what the killer would be wearing when they arrested him, and although he was caught at home late at night, wearing his pajamas, when police asked him to dress, he emerged from his room wearing a double-breasted suit, exactly as Brussel had predicted.)

"What is this force that takes a hold of a person and pushes them over the edge?" wondered Ressler, who interviewed scores of killers over the course of his illustrious career.

In an effort to infiltrate the minds of serial killers, Douglas and Ressler embarked on a mission to interview some of the most deranged serial killers in the country, starting their journey in California, which "has always had more than its share of weird and spectacular crimes," Douglas said.

In their search for a pattern, they determined that there are essential two types of serial killers: organized and disorganized.

Organized killers

Organized killers were revealed through their crime scenes, which were neat, controlled and meticulous, with effort taken both in the crime and with their victims. Organized killers also take care to leave behind few clues once they're done.

Dean Corll was an organized serial killer. He tortured his victims overnight, carefully collecting blood and bodily fluids on a sheet of plastic before rolling them up and burying them and their possessions, most beneath the floor of a boat shed he'd rented, going there late at night under the cover of darkness.

Disorganized killers

On the flip side of the coin, disorganized killers grab their victims indiscriminately, or act on the spur of the moment, allowing victims to collect evidence beneath their fingernails when they fight back and oftentimes leaving behind numerous clues including weapons.

"The disorganized killer has no idea of, or interest in, the personalities of his victims," Ressler wrote in his book "Whoever Fights Monsters," one of several detailing his work as a criminal profiler. "He does not want to know who they are, and many times takes steps to obliterate their personalities by quickly knocking them unconscious or covering their faces or otherwise disfiguring them."

Cary Stayner – also known as the Yosemite Killer – became a disorganized killer during his last murder, which occurred on the fly when he was unable to resist a pretty park educator.

Lucky for other young women in the picturesque park, he left behind a wide range of clues, including four unmatched tire tracks from his aging 1979 International Scout.

"The crime scene is presumed to reflect the murderer's behavior and personality in much the same way as furnishings reveal the homeowner's character," Douglas and Ressler later wrote, expanding on their findings as they continued their interview sessions.

Serial killers think they're unique – but they're not

Dr. Helen Morrison – a longtime fixture in the study of serial killers who keeps clown killer John Wayne Gacy's brain in her basement (after Gacy's execution she sent the brain away for an analysis that proved it to be completely normal) – said that at their core, most serial killers are essentially the same.

While psychologists still haven't determined the motives behind what drives serial killers to murder, there are certain characteristics they have in common, said Morrison, who has studied or interviewed scores of serial killers and wrote about her experiences in "My Life Among the Serial Killers."

Most often men, serial killers tend to be talkative hypochondriacs who develop a remorseless addiction to the brutality of murder.

Too, they are able to see their victims as inanimate objects, playthings, of you will, around simply for their amusement.

Empathy? Not on your life.

"They have no appreciation for the absolute agony and terror and fear that the victim is demonstrating," said Morrison. "They just see the object in front of them. A serial murderer has no feelings. Serial killers have no motives. They kill only to kill an object."

In doing so, they satisfy their urges, and quiet the tumultuous turmoil inside of them.

"You say to yourself, 'How could anybody do this to another human being?'" Morrison said. "Then you realize they don't see them as humans. To them, it's like pulling the wings off a fly or the legs off a daddy longlegs.... You just want to see what happens. It's the most base experiment."

Nature vs. nurture?

For many serial killers, the desire to kill is as innate at their hair or eye color, and out of control, but most experts say that childhood trauma is an experience shared by them all.

In 1990, Colin Wilson and Donald Seaman conducted a study of serial killers behind bars and found that childhood problems were the most influential factors that led serial killers down their particular path of death and destruction.

Former FBI profiler Robert Ressler – who coined the terms serial killer and criminal profiling – goes so far as to say that 100 percent of all serial killers experienced childhoods that were not filled with happy memories of camping trips or fishing on the lake.

According to Ressler, of all the serial killers he interviewed or studied, each had suffered some form of abuse as a child - either sexual, physical or emotional abuse, neglect or rejection by parents or humiliation, including instances that occurred at school.

For those who are already hovering psychologically on edge due to unfortunate genetics, such events become focal points that drive a killer to act on seemingly insane instincts.

Because there is often no solid family unit – parents are missing or more focused on drugs and alcohol, sexual abuse goes unnoticed, physical abuse is commonplace – the child's development becomes stunted, and they can either develop deep-seeded rage or create for themselves a fantasy world where everything is perfect, and they are essentially the kings of their self-made castle.

That was the world of Jeffrey Dahmer, who recognized his need for control much later, after hours spent in analysis where he learned the impact of a sexual assault as a child as well as his parents' messy, rage-filled divorce.

"After I left the home, that's when I started wanting to create my own little world, where I was the one who had complete control," Dahmer said. "I just took it way too far."

Dahmer's experiences suggest that psychopathic behavior likely develops in childhood, when due to neglect and abuse, children revert to a place of fantasy, a world where the victimization of the child shifts toward others.

"The child becomes sociopathic because the normal development of the concepts of right and wrong and empathy towards others is retarded because the child's emotional and social development occurs within his self-centered fantasies. A person can do no wrong in his own world and the pain of others is of no consequence when the purpose of the fantasy world is to satisfy the needs of one person," according to one expert.

As the lines between fantasy and reality become blurred, fantasies that on their own are harmless become real, and monsters like Dean Corll find themselves strapping young boys down to a wooden board, raping them, torturing them and listening to them scream, treating the act like little more than a dissociative art project that ends in murder.

Going inside the mind: Psychopathy and other mental illnesses

While not all psychopaths are serial killers – many compulsive killers do feel some sense of remorse, such as Green River Killer Gary Ridgeway did when he cried in court after one victim's father offered Ridgeway his forgiveness – those who are, Morrison said, are unable to feel a speck of empathy for their victims.

Their focus is entirely on themselves and the power they are able to assert over others, especially so in the case of a psychopath.

Psychopaths are charming — think Ted Bundy, who had no trouble luring young women into his car by eliciting sympathy with a faked injury — and have the skills to easily manipulate their victims, or in some cases, their accomplices.

Dean Corll was called a Svengali — a name taken from a fictional character in George du Maurier's 1895 novel "Trilby" who seduces, dominates and exploits the main character, a young girl — for being able to enlist the help of several neighborhood boys who procured his youthful male victims without remorse, even when the teens were their friends.

Some specific traits of serial killers, determined through years of profiling, include:

- **Smooth talking but insincere.** Ted Bundy was a charmer, the kind of guy that made it easy for people to be swept into his web. "I liked him immediately, but people like Ted can fool you completely," said Ann Rule, author of the best-selling "Stranger Beside Me," about her experiences with Bundy, a man she considered a friend. "I'd been a cop, had all that psychology — but his mask was perfect. I say that long acquaintance can help you know someone. But you can never be really sure. Scary."
- **Egocentric and grandiose.** Jack the Ripper thought the world of himself, and felt he would outsmart police, so much so that he sent letters taunting the London

officers. "Dear Boss," he wrote, "I keep on hearing the police have caught me but they won't fix me just yet. I have laughed when they look so clever and talk about being on the right track. That joke about Leather Apron gave me real fits. I am down on whores and I shan't quit ripping them till I do get buckled. Grand work the last job was. I gave the lady no time to squeal. How can they catch me now? I love my work and want to start again. You will soon hear of me with my funny little games. I saved some of the proper red stuff in a ginger beer bottle over the last job to write with but it went thick like glue and I can't use it. Red ink is fit enough I hope ha. ha. The next job I do I shall clip the lady's ears off and send to the police officers … My knife's so nice and sharp I want to get to work right away if I get a chance. Good luck."

- **Lack of remorse or guilt.** Joel Rifkin was filled with self-pity after he was convicted of killing and dismembering at least nine women. He called his conviction a tragedy, but later, in prison, he got into an argument with mass murderer Colin Ferguson over whose killing spree was more important, and when Ferguson taunted him for only killing women, Rifkin said, "Yeah, but I had more victims."

- **Lack of empathy.** Andrei Chikatilo, who feasted on bits of genitalia both male and female after his kills, thought nothing of taking a life, no matter how torturous it was for his victims. "The whole thing - the cries, the blood, the agony - gave me relaxation and a certain pleasure," he said.

- **Deceitful and manipulative.** John Wayne Gacy refused to take responsibility for the 28 boys buried beneath his house, even though he also once said that clowns can get away with murder. "I think after 14 years under truth serum had I committed the crime I would have known it," said the man the neighbors all claimed to like. "There's got to be something that would... would click in my mind. I've had photos of 21 of the victims and I've looked at them all over the years here and I've never recognized anyone of them."

- **Shallow emotions.** German serial killer Rudolph Pliel, convicted of killing 10 people and later took his own life in prison, compared his "hobby" of murder to playing cards, and later told police, "What I did is not such a great harm, with all these surplus women nowadays. Anyway, I had a good time."

- **Impulsive.** Tommy Lynn Sells, who claimed responsibility for dozens of murders throughout the Midwest and South, saw a woman at a convenience store and followed her home, an impulse he was unable to control. He waited until the house went dark, then "I went into this house. I go to the first bedroom I see...I don't know whose room it is and, and, and, and I start stabbing." The victim was the woman's young son.

- **Poor behavior controls**. "I wished I could stop but I could not. I had no other thrill or happiness," said UK killer Dennis Nilsen, who killed at least 12 young men via strangulation, then bathed and dressed their bodies before disposing of them, often by burning them.

- **Need for excitement.** For Albert Fish - a masochistic killer with a side of sadism that included sending a letter to the mother of one of his victims, describing in detail how he cut, cooked and ate her daughter - even the idea of his own death was one he found particularly thrilling. "Going to the electric chair will be the supreme thrill of my life," he said.

- **Lack of responsibility.** "I see myself more as a victim rather than a perpetrator," said Gacy, in a rare moment of admitting the murders. "I was cheated out of my childhood. I should never have been convicted of anything more serious than running a cemetery without a license. They were just a bunch of worthless little queers and punks."

- **Early behavior problems.** "When I was a boy I never had a friend in the world," said German serial killer Heinrich Pommerencke, who began raping and murdering girls as a teen.

- **Adult antisocial behavior.** Gary Ridgeway pleaded guilty to killing 48 women, mostly prostitutes, who were easy prey and were rarely reported missing – at least not immediately. "I don't believe in man, God nor Devil. I hate the whole damned human race, including myself... I preyed upon the weak, the harmless and the unsuspecting. This lesson I was taught by others: Might makes right."

'I felt like it'

Many psychopaths will say after a crime, "I did it because I felt like it," with a certain element of pride.

That's how BTK killer Dennis Rader felt, and because he had no sense of wrong regarding his actions, he was able to carry on with his normal life with his wife and children with ease.

Someone else's demeanor might have changed, they may have become jittery or anxious, and they would have been caught.

Many serial killers are so cold they are can pop into a diner right after a murder, never showing a sign of what they've done.

"Serial murderers often seem normal," according to the FBI. "They have families and/or a steady job."

"They're so completely ordinary," Morrison added. "That's what gets a lot of victims in trouble."

That normalcy is often what allows perpetrators to get away with their crimes for so long.

Unlike mass murderers such as terrorists who generally drop off the radar before perpetrating their event, serial killers blend in. They might seem a bit strange – neighbors noticed that Ed Gein wasn't too big on personal hygiene, and neighbors did think it was odd that William Bonin hung out with such young boys - but not so much so that anyone would ask too many questions.

"That's why so many people often say, "I had no idea" or "He was such a nice guy" after a friend or neighbor is arrested.

And it's also why people are so very, very stunned when they see stories of serial killers dominating the news.

"For a person with a conscience, Rader's crimes seem hideous, but from his point of view, these are his greatest accomplishments and he is anxious to share all of the wonderful things he has done," said Jack Levin, PhD, director of the Brudnick Center on Violence and Conflict at Northeastern University in Boston and the author of "Extreme Killings."

A new take on psychopathy

Psychopathy is now diagnosed as antisocial personality disorder, a prettier spin on an absolutely horrifying diagnosis.

According to studies, almost 50 percent of men in prison and 21 percent of women in prison have been diagnosed with antisocial personality disorder.

Of serial killers, Ted Bundy (who enjoyed sex with his dead victims), John Wayne Gacy and Charles Manson (who encouraged others to do his dirty work which included the murder of pregnant Sharon Tate) were all diagnosed with this particular affliction, which allowed them to carry out their crimes with total disregard toward others or toward the law.

They showed no remorse.

Schizophrenia

Many known serial killers were later diagnosed with some other form of mental illness, including schizophrenia, believed to be behind the crimes of David Berkowitz (he said his neighbor's dog told him to kill his six victims in the 1970s), Ed Gein, whose grisly saving of skin, bones and various female sex parts was a desperate effort to resurrect his death mother and Richard Chase (the vampire of Sacramento, who killed six people in California in order to drink their blood).

Schizophrenia includes a wide range of symptoms, ranging from hallucinations and delusions to living in a catatonic state.

Borderline personality disorder

Borderline personality disorder – which is characterized by intense mood swings, problems with interpersonal relationships and impulsive behaviors – is also common in serial killers.

Some diagnosed cases of borderline personality disorder include Aileen Wuornos, a woman whose horrific childhood and numerous sexual assaults led her to murder one of her rapists, after which she spiraled out of control and killed six other men who picked her up along with highway in Florida, nurse Kristen H. Gilbert, who killed four patients at a Virginia hospital with overdoses of epinephrine, and Dahmer, whose murder count rose to 17 before he was caught.

With a stigma still quite present regarding mental illness, it's likely we will continue to diagnose serial killers and mass murderers after the fact, too late to protect their victims.

Top signs of a serial killer

While there is still no simple thread of similarities – which is why police and the FBI have more trouble in real life solving crimes than they do on shows like "Criminal Minds" – there are some things to look for, experts say.

- **Antisocial Behavior.** Psychopaths tend to be loners, so if a child that was once gregarious and outgoing becomes shy and antisocial, this could be an issue.

Jeffrey Dahmer was a social, lively child until his parents moved to Ohio for his father's new job. There, he regressed – allegedly after being sexually molested – and began focusing his attentions on dissecting road kill rather than developing friendships.

- **Arson.** Fire is power, and power and control are part of the appeal for serial killers, who enjoy having their victims at their mercy. David Berkowitz was a pyromaniac as a child – his classmates called him Pyro as a nickname, so well-known was he for his fire obsession - and he reportedly started more than 1,000 fires in New York before he became the Son of Sam killer.

- **Torturing animals.** Serial killers often start young, and test boundaries with animals including family or neighborhood pets. According to studies, 70 percent of violent offenders have episodes of animal abuse in their childhood histories, compared to just 6 percent of nonviolent offenders. Albert DeSalvo – better known as the Boston Strangler – would capture cats and dogs as a child and trap them in boxes, shooting arrows at the defenseless animals for sport.

- **A troubled family history.** Many serial killers come from families with criminal or psychiatric histories or alcoholism. Edmund Kemper killed his grandparents to see what it would be like, and later – after he murdered a string of college students – he killed his alcoholic mother, grinding her vocal chords in the garbage disposal in an attempt to erase the sound of her voice.

- **Childhood abuse.** William Bonin – who killed at least 21 boys and young men in violent rapes and murders – was abandoned as a child, sent to live in a group home where he himself was sexually assaulted. The connections suggest either a rage that can't be erased – Aileen Wuornos, a rare female serial killer, was physically and sexually abused throughout her childhood, resulting in distrust of others and a pent-up rage that exploded during a later rape - or a disassociation of sorts, refusing to connect on a human level with others for fear of being rejected yet again.

- **Substance abuse.** Many serial killers use drugs or alcohol. Jeffrey Dahmer was discharged from the Army due to a drinking problem he developed in high school, and he used alcohol to lure his victims to his apartment, where he killed them in a fruitless effort to create a zombie-like sex slave who would never leave him.

- **Voyeurism.** When Ted Bundy was a teen, he spent his nights as a Peeping Tom, hoping to get a glimpse of one of the neighborhood girls getting undressed in their bedrooms.

- **Serial killers are usually smart.** While their IQ is not usually the reason why serial killers elude police for so long, many have very high IQs. Edmund Kemper was thisclose to being considered a genius (his IQ was 136, just four points beneath the 140 mark that earns genius status), and he used his intelligence to create complex cons that got him released from prison early after killing his grandparents, allowing eight more women to die.

- **Can't keep a job.** Serial killers often have trouble staying employed, either because their off-hours activities take up a lot of time (Jeffrey Dahmer hid bodies in his shower, the shower he used every morning before work, because he was killing at such a fast rate) or because their obsessions have them hunting for victims when they should be on the clock.

Trademarks of a serial killer

While what we know helps us get a better understanding of potential serial killers – and perhaps take a closer look at our weird little neighbors – it is still tricky for police and FBI agents to track serial killers down without knowing a few tells.

The signature

While serial killers like to stake a claim over their killings – "Serial killers typically have some sort of a signature," according to Dr. Scott Bonn, a professor at Drew University in New Jersey – they are usually still quite neat, and a signature does not necessarily mean evidence.

"Jack the Ripper, of course, his signature was the ripping of the bodies," said Bonn.

While there are multiple theories, Jack the Ripper has yet to be identified, despite the similarities in his murders.

Too, the Happy Face Killer, Keith Hunter Jespersen – whose childhood was marked by alcoholic parents, teasing at school and a propensity to abuse small animals - drew happy faces on the numerous letters he sent to both media and authorities, teasing them a bit with a carrot on a string.

"If the forensic evidence itself - depending upon the bones or flesh or whatever is left - if it allows for that sort of identification, that would be one way of using forensic evidence to link these murders," Bonn said.

The cooling off period

Organized killers are so neat, tidy and meticulous that they may never leave clues, even if they have a signature.

And if there's a long cooling off period between crimes, tracking the killer becomes even more of a challenge.

After a murder – which could be compared to a sexual experience or getting high on drugs – the uncontrollable urges that led the killer to act dissipate, at least temporarily.

But according to Ressler, serial killers are rarely satisfied with their kills, and each one increases desire – in the same way a porn addiction can start with the pages of Playboy then turn into BDSM videos or other fetishes when Playboy pictorials are no longer satisfying.

"I was literally singing to myself on my way home, after the killing. The tension, the desire to kill a woman had built up in such explosive proportions that when I finally pulled the trigger, all the pressures, all the tensions, all the hatred, had just vanished, dissipated, but only for a short time," said David Berkowitz, better known as the Son of Sam.

Afterwards, the memory of the murder, or mementos from the murder such as the skulls Jeffrey Dahmer retained, the scalps collected by David Gore or the box of vulvas Ed Gein kept in his kitchen, no longer become enough, and the killers must kill again, creating a "serial" cycle.

That window between crimes usually becomes smaller, however, which allows authorities to notice similarities in murder scenes or methodology, making tracking easier.

In the case of William Bonin, there were months between his first few murders, but toward the end, he sometimes killed two young men a day to satisfy his increasingly uncontrollable urges.

"Sometimes... I'd get tense and think I was gonna go crazy if I couldn't get some release, like my head would explode. So I'd go out hunting. Killing helped me... It was like ... needing to go gambling or getting drunk. I had to do it," Bonin said.

Hunting in pairs

Some serial killers – between 10 and 25 percent - find working as a team more efficient, and they use their charm as the hook to lure in accomplices.

Ed Gein may never have killed anyone had his accomplice, a mentally challenged man who helped Gein dig up the graves of women who resembled his mother, not been sent to a nursing home, leaving Gein unable to dig up the dead on his own.

Texas killer Dean Corll used beer, drugs, money and candy to bribe neighborhood boys to bring him their friends for what they were promised was a party, but instead would turn to torture and murder. He would have killed many more if one of his accomplices had not finally shot him to prevent another night of death.

William Bonin also liked to work with friends, and he enticed boys who were reportedly on the low end of the IQ scale to help him sadistically rape and torture his victims.

Other red flags

According to the FBI's Behavioral Science Unit – founded by Robert Ressler - 60 percent of murderers whose crimes involved sex were childhood bed wetters, and sometimes carried the habit into adulthood. One such serial killer, Alton Coleman, regularly wet his pants, earning the humiliating nickname "Pissy."

Sexual arousal over violent fantasies during puberty can also play a role in a serial killer's future.

Jeffrey Dahmer hit puberty about the same time he was dissecting road kill, so in some way, his wires became crossed and twisted, and sex and death aroused him.

Brain damage? Maybe

While Helen Morrison's test found that John Wayne Gacy's brain was normal, and Jeffrey Dahmer's father never had the opportunity to have his son's brain studied, although both he and Jeffrey had wanted the study, there is some evidence that some serial killers have brain damage that impact their ability to exact rational control.

"Normal parents? Normal brains? I think not," said Dr. Jonathan Pincus, a neurologist and author of the book "Base Instincts: What Makes Killers Kill."

"Abusive experiences, mental illnesses and neurological deficits interplayed to produce the tragedies reported in the newspapers. The most vicious criminals have also been, overwhelmingly, people who have been grotesquely abused as children and have paranoid patterns of thinking," said Pincus in his book, adding that childhood traumas can impact the developmental anatomy and functioning of the brain.

***

So what do we know?

Serial killers can be either uber-smart or brain damaged, completely people savvy or totally awkward, high functioning and seemingly normal or unable to hold down a job.

But essentially, no matter what their back story, their modus operandi or their style, "they're evil," said criminal profiler Pat Brown.

And do we need to know anything more than that?

A Note From The Author

Hello, this is Jack Rosewood. Thank you for reading Christopher Wilder: The True Story of The Beauty Queen Killer. I hope you enjoyed the read of this chilling story. If you did, I'd appreciate if you would take a few moments to post a review on Amazon.

I would also love if you'd sign up to my newsletter to receive updates on new releases, promotions and a FREE copy of my Herbert Mullin E-Book, www.JackRosewood.com

Best Regards
Jack Rosewood

www.ingramcontent.com/pod-product-compliance
Lightning Source LLC
LaVergne TN
LVHW021136300625
815018LV00010B/515